RECLAIMING LOVE:

Connecting the Head and the Heart

Fr. Martin Connor, LC

Copyright © 2020 RCSpirituality Center

Scriptures taken from New Revised Standard Version, copyright © 1989, Division of Christian Education of the National Council of the Churches of Christ in the United States of America.

Cover design by Ana Gutowski

ISBN: 9798644299140

To my father Paul Connor, Sr. (1925 - 2001) and my mother, Jean, his beloved wife of 47 years.

"As your love is, so are you."
St. Augustine

ACKNOWLEDGMENTS

With deep gratitude I acknowledge first Jen Settle from the Theology of the Body Institute who encouraged me to choose this theme for my thesis project back in 2014. I thank my brother priests, the lay family Regnum Christi, and the many friends who supported the efforts of this book. In particular, I want to recognize those who spent many hours reading and giving feedback for the final draft: Kelli Byrne, Ana Gutowski, Alexandra Cathey, Paula Barrenechea, Jimmy Mitchell, Janet McLaughlin, Fr. Bruce Wren, LC, Alicia de Olano, and Fr. Justin Kielhorn, LC. Many thanks also to Divine Mercy University, particularly Alexandra Marcotte, Christina McShane, and Fr. Robert Presutti, LC, who offered their insights into the psychological and healing elements of this work.

TABLE OF CONTENTS

Foreword xi
Introduction xv
Chapter One: Two Words – Emotions and Chastity 1
   St. John Paul II and Emotional Chastity 3
   Self-Possession 4
   The Feelings Revolution 6
   Living Emotional Chastity 7
Chapter Two: Who Am I? 13
   Human Dignity 13
   The Higher Purpose: Love 14
   Human Reason 16
   The Will 19
   How Reason and Will Work Together 20
   Freedom 22
   Conscience 25
   Moral Beings 28
   Human Sexuality 31
Chapter Three: Our Emotional World 37
   The Place of Emotions in the Human Person 37
   Emotions: What Do I Do with Them? 39

The Case of Anger..42
The Uniqueness of Shame.. 44
Emotions and the Heart... 48
Heart-Intuition 50
Love Doesn't Always "Feel" Good..52

Chapter Four: Progression of Love....................................57
First Stage: Love as Attraction... 58
Second Stage: Love as Desire 62
Third Stage: Love as Goodwill.. 68
Fourth Stage: Love as Unconditional..71
Conclusion of Stages of Love 76

Chapter Five: What Love Is NOT 79

Chapter Six: What Inhibits Living Emotional Chastity?..85
Human Frailty.. 85
Dehumanizing Secular Culture 89
The Reality of Evil 97

Chapter Seven: Redemption... 101

Chapter Eight: Living Emotional Chastity–The Law of Gradualness 107
Personal Reflection.. 108
Sacramental Life... 112
Life-Giving Relationships 114
Life-Giving Behavior 117
The Power of Intentional Gratitude 118

Epilogue 121
   Regnum Christi and Integral Formation 121
Key Terms and Definitions 125
Answers to Small Group Questions: 129
Appendices 149
   Appendix I: Helpful Tips for Silence 151
   Appendix II: Thought Management 153

FOREWORD

"He was in love with love".[1] The future Pope John Paul II, Karol Wojtyla, as a young priest spent hours with young people talking about love. He was in love with the experience of love itself. So important and so transforming was his experience of love that he made reflecting on it his life's work. My own studies of his reflections on love inspired me to spend the last five-plus years doing the same.

Surrounded and troubled by a world confused about this word "love," I set out to discover from others the meaning of love – young people, married couples, priests and consecrated men and women, persons from all walks of life. We discussed, we argued, we laughed, and we discussed some more. To the many individuals and couples who spent those hours with me, thank you! Coming to know love, to reclaim its true and most authentic expression, is so worth it. This book is the fruit of our conversations.

This book is also meant to be a platform for convinced believers, or as I call them, "kingdom builders." It is a small-group resource for those persons who desire to better accompany seekers of authentic love. These seekers are tired of empty and superficial relationships, desiring purposefulness and deeper

---

[1] These words that describe St. John Paul are echoed by the great sinner, convert to the Catholic faith now St. Augustine: "*To Carthage I came, where there sang all around me in my ears a cauldron of unholy loves. I loved not yet, yet I loved to love*" *(amans amare).* Augustine, Confessions, translation F. Sheed (New York: Sheed and Ward, 1965), Book 3.

meaning in their lives. We all want to be capable of great love in our life, at all levels of our relationships, from God to family, and especially with that special someone. Yet we need the wisdom of others to continue striving in this most important task. When we slow down enough to share such significant life topics with one another, everyone benefits and grows. This is a journey that is meant to be done with others: friends, family, acquaintances, married couples, single men and women, and consecrated persons. I hope the following reflections will be a helpful support in making this journey of the heart as personal and experiential as possible.

For two thousand years, Jesus Christ has been a model of unconditional love to an untold number of human beings. I was called by Jesus Christ to follow him with my life. Many will not understand this. Jesus Christ is not some distant historical character, inspiring ethical role model, or sentimental consolation for our times of difficulty. No! Christ is a real, living person. I will say only this: dead men do not call. Christ does call. He is our brother and friend, our best friend. He called me just like he called the first Apostles and he continues to call and model the way of love.

We live in a society which is pluralistic, and where there are disagreements about basic issues. I am not asking anyone to believe what I say in this book. I ask only that the reader examine the themes laid out here and discuss them with a group of trusted friends. Only by thinking through where we are now with this theme of love, and then going deeper into others' experiences, are we in a position to aspire to live authentic love in our lives in an ever more perfect way. This is our most important mission in life: *to love well*!

> **Special note to small group leaders:**
>
> This book is meant to generate personal discussion in your small group. It will be important for you to keep this very much in mind as you facilitate the discussion and lead your small group. You are encouraged to personalize the conversation by inserting your own experiences and drawing out of the participants their own experiences of the different themes presented here. Your role is to encourage an engaging conversation about the theme of love.
>
> Other resources to help facilitate your discussion:
> - "Going Deeper": Points to invite the small group to a more personal conversation, at the end of each section.
> - "Key Terms and Definitions" in the back of the book.
> - "Answers to Small Group Questions" in the back of the book.

INTRODUCTION

"Never had much faith in love or miracles
Never wanna put my heart on the line
But swimming in your world is something spiritual
I'm born again every time you spend the night
Cause your sex takes me to paradise
Yeah your sex takes me to paradise
And it shows, yeah, yeah, yeah
Cause you make me feel like, I've been locked out of heaven
For too long, for too long"

The words of Bruno Mars's popular song *Locked Out of Heaven* depict some fundamental truths about human love: It's charged with emotion, it's spiritual, and it can be a glimpse of heaven. The problem is that, at times, his lyrics mistakenly seem to reduce love to lust. However promising disordered love appears, it always seems to leave us dissatisfied, craving more excitement, never resting in the love of our beloved—hence the title "Locked Out of Heaven"! What is God's intention for human love? What is genuine love? What is ultimate fulfillment?

God's intention for human love is that it seeks satisfaction—not satisfaction merely in physical connection, but satisfaction in *human* connection which then leads ultimately to Divine connection. In other words, we human beings are more than just bodies. Genuine human love should connect us to another *person* through everything that makes us human: our senses, our emotions, our reason, our choices, our goals, and our dreams—and not just the high of physical pleasure. Love flows from the state of our mind and heart as human *persons*—not just as physical *bodies*. We find fulfillment when we learn to love with our whole selves. We find *ultimate* fulfillment when we learn to love like God calls us to love: "with all your heart, all your soul, and all your mind" (Matthew 22:37). And ultimately, we find complete fulfillment in heaven.

Today's society is told that the "hookup culture" is normal, and that one can disconnect emotions from physical forms of affection. Maybe we should pause and ask ourselves, "Is this true?"

Experience shows we cannot disconnect our core selves from our bodies, whether we think we can or not. We are one complete unit—mind, body, and soul—and *together* the whole "human package" is good. We are good because we have dignity as persons and not as things. Each of us desire to be respected and honored—not to be objectified and used, as we see so often today, resulting in pain and loneliness.

Love becomes *fully* human when the head and heart work together with one's body. Emotional chastity is the habit that harmonizes the head and heart, and directs them toward the good of the other, in order to love authentically. It seeks to bring the *"whole of me"* to love. This habit flows from a clear understanding of the worth of the other (head) so as to choose genuine love (heart) as a gift of the self to the other person. The gift of *the whole* self, head and heart, makes love fully human and brings true fulfillment. It is through the giving of ourselves that we discover ourselves.[2]

This book is about discovering what makes human love unique and beautiful, especially when it involves the whole person. It

---
[2] Vatican II documents, *Gaudium et Spes* (Northport, NY: Costello Publishing, 1975), 24.

hopes to explore human love in general, while highlighting the love between a man and a woman.

Let's dive deeper into human love and look at emotional chastity.

CHAPTER ONE: TWO WORDS – EMOTIONS AND CHASTITY

Emotions. Chastity. Emotional chastity. What are these? To fully understand emotional chastity, it is important to define each word on its own and to know their current cultural sense.

First, emotions are the psychic movements within the human person which produce motion and energy to help us in life. They are aspects of our human nature that aid us in living a fully human life and deepen how we love. A healthy and balanced emotional life should lead to a healthy capacity to love. A more in-depth discussion on emotions from this perspective will follow.

How does our culture view human emotions? On the one hand, it affirms that we listen to our emotions and see them almost as intuitive powers, like the "force" in Star Wars. In this case, doing away with caution is justified and leads quite quickly to thinking, saying, or doing whatever you feel. The 2017 Disney movie *Coco* illustrates this well. In it, the 13-year-old character, Miguel, feels emotionally attached to his music to the point of being obsessive and disregarding people around him. He is so enveloped in it that he blocks out the world in order to play his heart out! Another example might be a young girl who falls in love with an abusive boyfriend and despite the warnings of friends and family, she follows her "heart" and continues this dangerous relationship.

On the other hand, our culture can view emotions as a sign of weakness and immaturity. So often we see our culture emphasizing two extremes: ignored and unbridled. "Men, put away your emotions and never cry" and "women, unleash your emotions; we know you can't control them anyway!" The reflections in this book challenge us to find the happy medium.

So now let's talk about chastity.

To love is the most important choice in daily life. In order to love authentically, we need virtues or good habits that help us put the good of the other over our own good. Chastity is precisely the virtue that fosters a collaboration of the head and heart so as to choose to love authentically. This is why chastity is described as bringing unity to the person's bodily and spiritual being.[3] It is about respecting ourselves first, so then we can respect the other we love.

How does our culture view chastity? There is much misunderstanding today around the word chastity. Some have never heard of it. Others mistakenly believe it is the repression of our desires or emotions to conform to outdated moral rules. However, a right understanding of chastity does *not* include rejection of human love, isolation, or prudery, but rather includes a joyful and free expression of human love. It enables us to *freely choose* how we respond to the person we love. Chastity *is* freedom. Chastity frees us from the tendency to use the other for personal gratification.

More on the word's emotions and chastity later, but now let's go a bit deeper into the concept of emotional chastity.

Small Group Questions:
1. Define in your own words: emotions and chastity.
2. In your own experience, how does our culture view emotions? How does it view chastity? Give examples.

---

[3] *Catechism of the Catholic Church* (*CCC*) (New York: Doubleday, 1995), 2337.

St. John Paul II and Emotional Chastity

From where does the term emotional chastity come? Much of what is written about emotional chastity today is inspired by the teachings of St. John Paul II. He was elected pope in 1978, served until his death in 2005, and was canonized a saint in 2014. His teaching on marriage and family have revolutionized our modern-day perspective on human sexuality. Though he never used the exact term "emotional chastity" in his writings, St. John Paul II called for a rehabilitation of the meaning of the virtue called chastity both before and after his election as pope.[4]

St. John Paul II said that love is self-gift, that is, a *whole* person freely giving himself to another: body *and* soul. His efforts to explore a more complete definition of human love led some of his followers to coin the term *emotional chastity*.[5] This term expresses how healthy love involves both the head and the heart. It is *not* the suppression of our emotions or desire (even sexual desire); rather, it is the total orientation of one's life towards a goal to love well.[6]

Emotional chastity is the habit that harmonizes the head and heart, and directs them towards the good of the other, in order to love authentically.

Small Group Questions:
1. What does St. John Paul II mean when he says that love is self-gift?
2. What is emotional chastity and where does the word come from?

---

[4] Karol Wojtyla, *Love and Responsibility* (San Francisco: Ignatius Press, 1993), 143-147.
[5] Some of the authors and speakers on this theme are Ed Sri, Sara Swafford, and Jason Evert.
[6] *CCC* 2337. "Chastity means the successful integration of sexuality within the person....sexuality becomes...personal and truly human...in the complete and lifelong mutual gift of a man and a woman."

Self-Possession

Loving with the head and heart begins with self-possession. Self possession is self knowledge, self acceptance, and self improvement. St. John Paul II said that in giving ourselves (self-gift), we must first possess ourselves, and then we will ultimately find ourselves.[7] So how do we possess ourselves? It is certainly not by casting blame on something or someone else. Nobody blames the hand that steals, or the mouth that speaks offensive words. Rather, self-possession implies two things: (1) personal ownership and (2) a responsibility toward the other.

Personal ownership speaks to our having full possession of our drives, passions, and motivations. Responsibility toward the other, rather, speaks to seeking the good of the other. It desires to serve that good without any hint of using the other for one's own sake. Love as a total gift of self, expressed through self-possession, is not a *what's in it for me* approach. It is a pure love. Emotional chastity flows out of self-possession. Self-possession empowers us to take responsibility for our own actions and for the good of others. Its core is untainted, pure love.

Healthy human love begins with self-possession because it seeks an *ordered* response to all our desires. It avoids the extreme. For example, consider our desire for food. When it comes to eating, could there be another option besides the extreme of gorging oneself (gluttony) or the other extreme of starving oneself (anorexia)? Of course, we choose it practically every day. Might it be the same with our sexual desire? Could there be another option besides the extreme of using another person for physical or emotional gratification separate from a loving relationship or the other extreme of refusing appropriate physical pleasure as wrong or immoral (prudery)? Of course, this is possible.

---

7   Cfr. Wojtyla, *Love and Responsibility*, 98.

Chapter One: Two Words – Emotions and Chastity

Self-possession is at the very root of the desire; from its very source there is balance and order.

Self-possession defends the essential value of the person from the extremes. Emotional chastity empowers one to use our human and sexual powers intelligently in the expression of love as self-gift. St. John Paul II's insights about self-possession attempt to recover the true and healthy expression of love in every state in life: the single life, the married life, and the celibate life of priests and consecrated persons.[8]

However, in the pervasiveness of our materialistic culture, we need to distinguish between true self-possession and false self-possession. Today one hears things like "my body is mine" and "I can do whatever I want with it," as if the body was separate from the rest of "me." It is a common practice to treat the body like any other material object to be owned, controlled, or possessed. This is false self-possession. Rather, the truth is, my body *is* me! How I treat my body is how I ultimately treat my very self, because we are one and the same! This profound truth is perfectly expressed by Crystalina Evert in *Pure Womanhood*:

> *"In high school, taking pregnancy tests scared me to death. The experience would freak me out for a while, but then I'd be back to my same old ways. Out of fear, I went on the birth control pill and later took the shot. But something happened to me every time I popped the pill or took the shot. I felt like part of me was dying. I suppose that when we disrespect our bodies in relationships, we become careless with our bodies in other ways. We even*

---

[8] One of the confusions today is the difference between celibacy and chastity: Celibacy is a promised state of singleness for the sake of the Kingdom of God, and hence not open to everyone. Chastity is a virtue that has always been understood as normative to live a Christian life—a healthy integrated sexuality—and hence it is for everyone.

> *begin to act against our bodies. It is like we start to separate ourselves from our bodies".*[9]

True self-possession, therefore, involves a deep awareness of the dignity of our "wholeness," our complete self-worth: body and soul. If in giving our whole selves we possess ourselves, then with confidence we can say that "when I love another person with no conditions, I become more human, more in fact, myself."[10]

Small Group Questions:
1. Discuss the words: "In giving ourselves, we must first possess ourselves, and then we will ultimately find ourselves."
2. Why does healthy human love begin with self-possession?
3. Distinguish true self-possession from false self-possession with concrete examples in your life.

The Feelings Revolution

Today there does not seem to be a lot of self-possession in relationships. We clearly see the dominance of raw human emotions particularly in the arena of love. This did not happen overnight. Among many possible causes, history points to what could be called "the feelings revolution" initiated by the famous Sigmund Freud in the early 1900s. Freud said that neurotic repression of our emotions and feelings is detrimental to our emotional health. There were some true positives from this philosophy: a greater openness of personal expression, improved parenting skills with more affirmation of the child's feelings, and the connection in the medical field between bodily

---

9   Chrystalina Evert, *Pure Womanhood* (Scottsdale, AZ: Totus Tuus Press, 2018), 22.
10 St. John Paul II called this "the interior freedom of the gift." See "Terms and Definitions" in the back of the book.

health and our emotional health.[11] However, from such considerations, disseminated now for almost a century, came the popular, yet unfounded belief that any form of *self-restraint* was an invitation to neuroses or forms of phobia. Despite the positives of Freud's theory, unfortunately, the negatives were felt far and wide, impacting every form of human relationship—from marriage and family dynamics to workplace realities. Encouraging human emotions to be shared at all times, uninhibited, uncontrolled, and unschooled is irresponsible, and even reckless.

Yet the greatest negative effect of the feelings revolution was expressed in the area of human sexuality, where emotions tend to be most consequential. The rejection of self-control as being unhealthy has led from mutual respect in human love to the disordered using of other people for personal pleasure. Add to this the accessibility and immediacy of the internet and social media, and a culture of instant emotional gratification has been born. It is a world that fosters little capacity to reflect on or discern behavior, but only to react to what one feels in the moment. Of course, this makes for a lot of bad choices, resulting in chaotic living which leads to disillusionment and unhappiness.

Small Group Questions:
1. Discuss the truth of the feelings revolution in the current culture.
2. Why would the greatest negative effect of the feelings revolution be expressed in human sexuality?

Living Emotional Chastity

Emotional chastity is about good choices, but good choices are just the start. It is more about the integrating effect of many

---
[11] Conrad W. Baars, *Feeling and Healing Your Emotions* (Plainfield, NJ: Logos International, 1979), 4-5.

good choices over time that nurtures one's capacity for the gift of self. It is about making the next good choice, then the next good choice, then the next, and these good choices culminate over time to help one's life and relationships become life-giving and healthy. This brings personal fulfillment. For example, imagine a young teenage girl who starts dating a guy. She notices that she is always trying to convince herself that it is okay to spend so much time with her boyfriend at the expense of her family and friends. This begins to stress her out. She remembers the advice of a trusted friend who said to her once, "Love brings peace, but lust brings angst." She resolves to speak to her boyfriend about physical boundaries and remind him of their mutual desire to save themselves for marriage. Again, it is not the single act of turning the ship in the right direction, but the ship itself going in the right direction as a result of past and ongoing good choices.

The building blocks of self-possession involve getting the head and heart, the whole person, to work together. It is a challenging pathway which attempts to free us from selfish attitudes towards other people. It requires maturity, a lived experience, and the continual free choice of self-restraint. By living emotional chastity, we will come to a deeper appreciation of our purpose and mission in life as stated in the Gospel of Mark: "to love with all our heart, with all our soul, with all our mind, and with all our strength, and to love one's neighbor as oneself" (Mark 12:30). This is truly our most important mission on earth: to love. St. John Paul II proclaimed this truth to the world in 1979:

> *"Man cannot live without love. He remains a being incomprehensible to himself, his life is senseless, if love is not revealed to him, if he does not encounter love."*[12]

---

[12] St. John Paul II, *Redeemer of Man* (Boston: Pauline Books and Media, 1991), 10.

Chapter One: Two Words – Emotions and Chastity

Yet who is going to show us the way to this encounter with love? This generation seeks mentors, life coaches, people who truly walk *the walk of love*. God is already ahead of us. We do have someone who will accompany us and promised us he will be with us. God has done us a great favor by sending us his Son, a person "like us in all things except sin" (Hebrews 4:15). We truly encounter love when we encounter love incarnate, the person of Jesus Christ. He is our model. He is the way. Indeed, for St. John Paul II, only Christ the Redeemer can fully reveal man to himself:

> *"If we wish to understand ourselves thoroughly, and not just in accordance with immediate or often superficial standards, we must with our unrest, uncertainty, and even our weakness and sinfulness draw near to Christ."*[13]

This encounter with Love Incarnate brings healing and real change of heart in our lives. Clearly from his own lived experience, St. John Paul II says:

> *"If this profound encounter with Love takes place within us, we then bear fruit not only of adoration of God but also of deep wonder at ourselves. We discover again the greatness, dignity, and value that belongs to our humanity. In the mystery of the God-man, Jesus Christ, we become newly "expressed" and, in a way, newly created. We are new creatures."*[14]

When we freely choose to partner with Christ and the power of his grace, then we can live an authentic love. Emotional chastity forges this authentic love for another, challenging us to love with our whole selves: with our head and with our heart.

---

13 Ibid.
14 Ibid.

Understanding what it means to be a human person and how to love is crucial for our lives. Chapter Two will explain our human makeup: dignity, purpose, reason, will, freedom, conscience, morality, and human sexuality. We will explore how they work together to produce healthy human love. For those just beginning this reflection and also this personal journey, I ask: If at the end of our lifetime, we will be judged on how we love, then how can there be any subject more important to understand, and then to live, than how we love?

Chapter Three will look at the emotional world in the human person. Chapter Four dives into how love progresses from mere instinctual attraction to mature self-gift love, concluding in Chapter Five with a clear description of what love is *not*. The factors today that hinder our ability to live out emotional chastity are explained in Chapter Six, and Chapter Seven offers hope and confidence in the help of God who heals and elevates our human brokenness to a more mature love. Finally, and with uncompromising honesty, Chapter VIII recognizes that progress along this path happens only gradually and with much patience. Genuine love fills our life with meaning and purpose, and this final chapter will give practical suggestions for living the art of love.

Small Group Questions:
1. Why is emotional chastity in the end all about good choices?
2. Why do we seek mentors or life coaches?

Going Deeper: Name a concrete situation in which the perspective of someone outside your family could be a great support.

NOTES

CHAPTER TWO: WHO AM I?

It is a good question, since identity confusion seems to reign all around us. The human person is unique, complex, and, in every sense, a gift. The next two chapters attempt to show this essential truth and will explore the key elements that make up a broad understanding of what it is to be human. It takes us from the natural elements of our human dignity, to our purpose in life, to the why of our sexuality, and finally to the exploration of our emotional world. By knowing better the nuts and bolts of being human, we will be highlighting just how important it is to develop a proper capacity to love with your whole self.

Human Dignity

The dignity of the human person occupies the very center of the teachings of St. John Paul II. Man is not merely an animal any more than man is merely a tree. He is a little world gathering all other worlds. Like plants, a man eats food, grows, and reproduces; and like animals, he feels pain and pleasure, and has instincts. These are his bodily, material characteristics. Like angels, and yet different, a man knows the truth and desires the good. These are his spiritual characteristics. We human beings are plant-like, animal-like, and angel-like; but we are not plants, animals, or angels.[15] We are human beings. We are persons. One author describes the uniqueness of being human in this way:

> *"I am significant because I am at the apex of the created order. I can think and choose, communicate my thoughts via words; I can know and understand history and learn from it. I experience death and sense there is existence beyond the material. I discover that in all peoples and*

---
15   Baars, *Feeling and Healing Your Emotions*, 6.

> cultures, people believe in a spiritual world, and my heart tells me it's true. There is a higher purpose."[16]

We have a higher purpose because we are made in the image of God. Two thousand years of Christian civilization have taught us that "man is a person, man and woman equally so, since both were created in the image and likeness of the personal God."[17] Our unique spiritual powers and our capacity for relationship image God. Our dignity flows from our ability to behave "in the image of God."

Small Group Questions:
1. What makes human beings unique from plants, animals, and angels?
2. Why do we have a higher purpose as human beings?

Going Deeper: Reflect as a group on the reality that each of us are unrepeatable and unique human beings.

The Higher Purpose: Love

God is love and created us to love. This is our special dignity and higher purpose: love. It is the fundamental and innate calling of every human being. St. John Paul II would call this the *unrepeatability and mystery* of each human person—the capacity to love and to be loved, each in our unique way.

Human love is about a relationship between persons because Divine love is *first* that way. God, as revealed by Jesus, is a Trinity, an intimate relationship of three persons (Father, Son, and Holy Spirit). One could say that the inner life of God is an

---

16 Gary Chapman, *Five Love Languages* (Chicago: Northfield Publishing, 1995), 155-56.
17 CCC 2334.

interpersonal relationship: one Divine person perfectly loving and receiving the love of the other. God is a communion of persons. As one writer states:

> *"Why do Christians believe in the Trinity? The answer is because they believe God is love... God is love in himself, because he has always had in himself a Son, the Word, whom he loves with an infinite love which is the Holy Spirit. In each love there are always three realities or subjects: one who loves, one who is loved, and the love which unites them."*[18]

The strongest evidence that we are made in the image of the Trinity is that love alone makes us happy. Because we live in relationships, we live to love and to be loved. A faith-based understanding of the human person takes its starting point in this Divine mystery[19] of the Creator. What God is, in himself, points to the inner calling of each of us as his creatures to be a gift to the other.

> *"God who created man out of love also calls him to love—the fundamental and innate vocation of every human being."*[20]

Small Group Questions:
1. Why did God create human beings?
2. What evidence do we have that we are made in the image of the Trinity?

Going Deeper: Discuss why it makes sense that we as creatures are literally "made for love."

---

[18] Raniero Cantalamessa, *Trinity Sunday Homily*, Zenit.org, June 9, 2006.
[19] Mary Prokes, *Toward a Theology of the Body* (New York: T&T Clark Ltd., 1996), 97.
[20] CCC 1604.

Human Reason

Human beings have the unique ability to reason. Animals do not. This is a significant distinction between humans and animals. For example, human beings can reflect on their lives and relationships; they can compose music; they can choose to love another person. Animals do not do any of these things because they do not have the capacity for it. We also can know truth by reason, like mathematical truths such as 2+2=4. There are also moral truths that are *universal*, meaning that all human beings are capable of knowing them; for example, the moral truth that it is never right to violate another human being. We *can know* these truths. Animals cannot. Our ability to reason does, in fact, define our differences from animals.

Current thinking, however, would like to eliminate these universal truths common to all, often leaving us in rational and moral confusion. It is true that there are striking differences between the ethical values of many particular cultures. Nevertheless, contemporary anthropology does show that there are basic universal truths, including respect for the value of life, begetting and raising of children, intellectual knowledge, and play or recreation. These universal truths run like permanent threads through all cultures. They are recognized universal values that are important and indeed fundamental to human life.[21] Human reason is not blind nor indifferent to these truths.

Our human reason, loosely speaking, has two mental-power sources that feed it so that we may understand the world around us. First, from the external material world, our mind processes, relates, analyzes, and judges what it receives through the senses to understand it. We can call this the discursive

---

[21] Germain Grisez and Russel Shaw, *Beyond the New Morality* (Notre Dame, IN: Notre Dame Press, 1980), 62. See also *Natural Law* in "Terms and Definitions" in the back of the book.

mind, and from this process, we acquire what is called discursive knowledge. We go from one mental step to the next. A simple example of this discursive knowledge is when we study a map, and all the pros and cons, before going on a trip. Our mind goes through a discursive reasoning process that helps us decide the best route to take.

The second mental-power source, which is much less known, comes without any effort from our reason. From this power source comes what we call intuition. For example, one might sit and ponder the beauty of an early morning sunset. This contemplation may inspire prayer. Our intuitive mind *perceives and receives* the power and awesomeness of creation at that moment, independent of any active reasoning process. Our intuitive mind receives its knowledge from sources such as nature, the arts, faith, or directly from God through the spirit. If the human person is said to be more than merely a material thing, "it is the intuitive mind that is the basis of his inner spiritual life and provides the link between the material and spiritual worlds."[22]

Unfortunately, modern philosophy has practically reduced all human understanding to discursive knowledge. This is the demise of the more passive, receptive intuition of our understanding. The great thinkers of antiquity thought otherwise, saying that our human understanding is both discursive and intuitive simultaneously.

The complete sum of our human knowledge is the action of the two together. This point is more important than one might think. Our Western culture seems to be in too much of a hurry to give a noble thing like contemplation a good try. Yet, from where have the numerous accomplishments of our technological age come? Often, they have come from a sudden insight

---

22   Baars, *Feeling and Healing Your Emotions*, 27.

received in a moment of quiet, in times when our reason was less active. Life is not all logic; it is not a problem to be solved, but a mystery to be lived.

In fact, it is imperative for our own mental health to take much needed "mental leisure" through non-active reflection like listening to beautiful music, taking walks in lovely settings, exposing our souls to encounter God through prayer. To bring home this point, I repeat one of the most important human truths we can know: the spiritual truths we receive from our intuitive minds grant us a happiness of a superior order (over that of the discursive mind). These spiritual truths that lie beyond our senses and rational observation—God, the soul, life after death, eternity, and others—are simply more important than the day-to-day worldly things that often consume us. They are of lasting interest to the human person.[23] Hence, the real challenge is to prioritize this form of mental leisure in our lives.

To summarize, both mental-power sources feed our understanding so we can know ourselves and the world around us. One source is more active (discursive); the other is more receptive (intuitive). In the end, human reason can be compared to a light. It illuminates and judges the right and true path that we should take, but has no way of moving us in this right direction. It needs a motor and this motor is the will.

Small Group Questions:
1. What human characteristic most distinguishes us from animals?
2. Name some objective truths that are universal for all people.
3. Discuss the differences between the two mental-power sources.

---

[23] Baars, *Feeling and Healing Your Emotions*, 30.

Going Deeper: Name a moment that you know in your life when too much thinking or rationalizing was bad for you. Name a moment when your "intuition" failed you.

The Will

Human beings also have the unique ability to choose freely. The faculty of our will is the motor that moves us down that pathway of choosing the good.[24] Our free will has the final word in making decisions and does so with the help of information provided by the light of reason. In the end, *the good* is what we desire in all our willing.[25] The good that the will chooses is what is loveable or desirable. It is that which engages and attracts our entire person.

The "good" of a person is closely related to "ought." "A good diet provides what a diet *ought* to provide; a good dad is a dad who does what a dad *ought* to do (of course different fathers have different views on what that is)."[26] "Ought" points to full, fuller, and fullest being, that is, the deep-down desire *to be* the finest possible human being. We value *this particular good* as helping us to be *more or better* persons, and we judge to be bad that which cuts off further possibilities for us.

Truly the simplest of choices of our will should engage the whole person, including our emotions. The psychologist Conrad Baars summarizes this well:

---

24 Thomas Aquinas, *Summa Theologica* (Chicago: Great Books of the Western World, Encyclopedia Britannica, Inc., 1990), Q.82 art. 4, reply obj. 1: "We can easily understand why these powers include one another in their acts, because the intellect understands that the will wills, and the will wills the intellect to understand."
25 Servais Pinkaers, *The Sources of Christian Ethics* (Washington, DC: CUA Press, 1995), 410.
26 Grisez and Shaw, *Beyond the New Morality*, 81.

> "Man's will is not the absolute and supreme principle of human conduct as was generally believed. The will was not to be trained to overcome and master our suspect and dangerous passions, but rather to rule them democratically, i.e., to listen to them respectfully and together with them strive for the good...moral good appeals not only to the will through reason but also directly to the emotions of love and desire through the senses."[27]

This is the right and positive outlook toward the value of our emotional life. It shows how a person can strive for the good when the light of reason works with our desires and will. Such a person can be said to have *real* willpower because his will is supported and motivated by the desire for the good.

Small Group Questions:
1. What are we seeking with our free choices?
2. What desire does "ought" point to?
3. How should the will respect the role of emotions?

How Reason and Will Work Together

Still, our will needs reason to see the good. The **will** is like a motor with no light and **reason** is like a light with no motor. Within each person, reason and will work together to "see" (reason) and to "move" (will) toward the right and true end. The light of reason is essential to illuminating and discerning "apparent goods" from "true goods" so that the will chooses correctly. Family, faith, and life experience educate both reason and will in what those proper goods are.

---

[27] Baars, *Feeling and Healing Your Emotions*, 70.

We can see the close integration of reason and will and how their education plays out when we analyze our experience of making a choice, for example, the choice of dating a person. The choice is basically directed by our desires to get to know the good of this other person. However, it is our reason that helps us move beyond the immediate physical or emotional attraction and wisely consider everything from family background, to personality, to common values. In the end, such thoughtful evaluation helps reason "see" and "move" the motor of the will to make the right choice. "Yes, this person is a *good* for me" or "no, this person is not right for me."

In the depths of every person, there is a sense of the true (reason) and the good (will), acting together and striving to incorporate our emotional world to choose the good. When these three dimensions (reason, will, emotions) are not integrated, the person can be enslaved. For example, when one is dominated by too much rationalizing or driven by too much emotion, this shows a lack of mature human integration that may lead to making harmful decisions. In the beginning, especially, the will is most important in helping us set our course that will allow the heart and head to work together. Nonetheless, when these three dimensions are active and cooperating, it is a joyful integration. The human person is truly free and flourishes.

Small Group Questions:
1. Why do reason and will need each other?
2. Why is it so important that our reason, will, and emotions are integrated?

Going Deeper: Have you personally experienced a time when you did not use reason and will together to make a decision and that decision turned out badly? Or the opposite when you did use reason and will together and made a great decision?

Freedom

The simultaneous and healthy integration of reason, will, and emotions make up authentic freedom. Freedom is a total gift from God and can have many different meanings.

Today, emphasis is given almost exclusively to that freedom called *freedom from restriction,* that is, from all things that might inhibit our capacity to choose whatever we want. The mere arbitrary power *to choose* appears to be the *essence* of this freedom. It is centered wholly on the fact that "I *can* choose whatever I want, whether it be good or evil." In other words, this freedom is *indifferent* to right and wrong. It is reduced to the free act of the person and emphasizes absolute personal autonomy. However, this apparent unconstrained freedom is impossible: human freedom will always have boundaries because we are finite, limited creatures. It is also a deception! This freedom from restrictions can perversely foster a license to do whatever pleases us, even if it is evil. It says, "All that matters is that I am free to act as I like, even if it is evil." How can this concept of freedom be good for any person or any community?

Sadly, we see a freedom to follow blind desire so often today, particularly in the domain of passionate love. For example, we may hear, "I had no choice," or "I was overwhelmed by the attraction," or "It felt right." The truth is that we *do* have a choice in the matter. Submitting to our passions in a given moment, at the expense of what our reason indicates is good for us, can lead us down a painful road. Just think of the countless unwanted pregnancies in our world, and the unnecessary pain, despair, and even death that such a reality can bring to human life. The "if it feels good, do it" mentality with no regard for consequences is a bold face lie! Of course, "we are free to choose what we will do. But we are not free to make whatever we choose **right**. We must follow our best judgment concerning what we ought to do, but our best judgment can be mistaken."[28]

Emotional chastity operates from a different concept of freedom: *freedom for excellence*. Freedom for excellence is rooted in our reason *and* our will together. Our natural inclination is to *know truth (reason)* and *choose it as good for us (will)*.[29]

Freedom for excellence requires allowing ourselves to "feel" fully, not suppressing our feelings. Reason acknowledges the feeling and brings us to that good which will most help us flourish. It also challenges us to understand the *power of choice* and how we form our own lives—in a sense, our own *selves*—through our choices.[30] This feeling, thinking, and choosing takes place on the level of personhood. It is what being human means.

Freedom for excellence bests reflects our dignity and self-respect because we are not reduced to acting on blind impulse nor mere external pressure.

This freedom for excellence is the foundational principle by which emotional chastity operates. It is about knowing and choosing a greater good through the power of one's emotional state. Ultimately, it frees us from that selfish dependency we may have on lesser, short-term goods, rather than on the goods that will bring long-term happiness. The total gift of self in love is *that ultimate good* which is, in the end, the best choice. Every time we choose self-gift love, we choose excellence because we are choosing what is best for another person and what is best for ourselves.

---

28   Grisez and Shaw, *Beyond the New Morality*, 59.
29   Pinkaers, *The Sources of Christian Ethics*, 393-94.
30   Grisez and Shaw, *Beyond the New Morality*, 1.

24   RECLAIMING LOVE

It is critical to point out that freedom for excellence, to know and choose a greater good, is not just something with which we are born. It is something we **achieve**. If the gift of self in love is the greatest good and the most excellent of choices, we will need to work hard to achieve it. It is not an automatic habit, because any habit demands dedication and consistency. Fulton Sheen put it well when he said:

> "We make ourselves free by knocking off all those hindrances and obstacles to the development and unfolding of what is highest in us—namely, the pursuit of Truth and Love and Goodness which is basically the definition of God. Freedom is not attainable at once, but by leaps and bounds. It is not a baby cradle from which we cry and pout, shriek and clamor for the satisfaction of our biological wants, but rather a hurdle race in which we surmount obstacles to win the race of being free on the inside."[31]

Love as self-gift is an arduous daily task. It can be likened to so many things in life: from learning to play an instrument, to excellence in sports, to learning another language. It takes dedication and training to acquire the skill! If you really want to be good at loving like this, then you need to practice, and practice a lot.

It is of great importance for us to understand freedom because authentic love must be free. If our love is somehow inhibited or even enslaved by something, then it is not true love—whether we are aware of this or not. A host of disordered desires and other selfish tendencies can enslave our love—depicted so well by the Crosby, Stills, and Nash song: "*If you can't be with the one you love, honey, love the one you're with.*" When the

---
31   Fulton Sheen, *On Being Human* (Garden City, New York: Image Books, 1983), 175.

attractions of lesser goods enslave us (when, for example, the physical attraction to another person overcomes our decision to remain faithful to a committed relationship), we are not free to choose the best good for us—leading our life to turmoil and ultimately to chaos.

If a free response of authentic love expresses our dignity and purpose, then it is truly the most important virtuous habit to live. To choose this love is to choose the most excellent thing!

Small Group Questions:
1. If freedom is a gift from God, then what do we mean by freedom from restrictions?
2. Why does authentic love need to be free?

Going Deeper: Can you think of a time where you lived freedom for excellence? What was it like?

Conscience

As persons, we also have the inner voice of conscience. Conscience is that secret core of the human heart: the messenger of God that bids the person, at the appropriate moment, to do good and to avoid evil.[32] The conscience is the practical judgment of our reason, judging a concrete action as either good or bad before, during, or after the action. The conscience "sees" the good and urges us to choose it, but it does not choose it for us. We are always free to choose. "Freedom of conscience is never freedom from the truth, but always and only freedom 'in' the truth."[33]

---

32 Vatican Council II, *Gaudium et Spes* (Northport, NY: Costello Publishing, 1975), 16.
33 St. John Paul II, *Splendor of Truth* (Boston: Pauline Books and Media, 1993), 64.

There are certain unwritten truths inscribed into our human fabric that will always be good for us. For example, take something so basic and simple as giving up your seat on a bus when someone elderly needs to sit. We do not create that standard of choice when it presents itself. It already exists. We could call it the inner law of *right* human behavior. We just know it is the right thing to do and our conscience points to it as "do this good." I am free to act or not on the voice of conscience when I see such an opportunity arise. Yet, other times the course of action is not so clear. Seeking to know and do the right thing, what is just and good, is called the education of the conscience.

When it comes to the gift of self in love, our conscience is educated through *witnessing to and participating in* such healthy life-giving relationships. Consistently this fact has proven true in the many I have counseled: Healthy family life = healthy love. The importance of good family relationships affirms the standard of that inner law of love in our conscience. St. John Paul II said:

> ..."*the family is the place where every human being appears in his or her uniqueness and unrepeatability. It is, and must be, a system of forces in which each member is important and necessary.*"[34]

Family or community life is that system of forces that reinforces the person we are becoming. If we tend to be selfish and unforgiving with others, like within our family, then such habits appear across the board in all our relationships. When the right standards are affirmed in the family consistently over time, they communicate that "*this is a good thing to do; this is how you treat another person,*" and it becomes habit. The healthy and consistent giving and receiving of love in family and friendship is the critical training ground for forming the habit of emotional

---
34 Wojtyla, *Love and Responsibility*, 305 (footnote no. 57).

chastity. For those who have not had a positive upbringing, or maybe come from a broken home, all is not lost. *Foundational relationships* that help transform us are always possible in life but must be sought out intentionally.

Our free choices can take us also in the opposite direction of what is just and good: selfishness. We know we want to be loved and cared for, but we may not be as good at acting this way towards others. We have the freedom to behave more like subhuman species than dignified reflective human beings. Damaged relationships and the self-centered collective culture around us can debunk the right standard of love every human being deserves—love as self-gift. Negative experiences can deform our conscience, so that it does not see and judge well. Hence, we can quite easily be inclined to see the other person as a means to our ends and fall into a mentality of using others. Nowhere else is this self-destructive way of thinking and acting seen more than in the arena of human love.

No one is born with a well-formed conscience. We educate that inner voice only through what attracts our attention. The gift of conscience is nourished with healthy sources of truth, goodness, and beauty; a good example is building friendships with people who love you and challenge you to be your best rather than accepting a weaker version of yourself. One writer sums up well the battle to form our conscience:

> *"Until we commit ourselves to listening to such quality sources and participating in such activities, our conscience may only reflect the shallow, passing age (Romans 12:1-2). This passing age, or the values of the popular Western culture, is transmitted through the media, politics, fashion, entertainment, and financial concerns. Such a conscience does not contain substantial*

enough nourishment to sustain a Catholic conscience, one that is directing you toward salvation and not simply toward "success" or "acceptance" in and by this age."[35]

This education of conscience is a lifelong task and engenders peace of heart.

Small Group Questions:
1. Define the word conscience. Must I listen to the voice of my conscience?
2. Why do family relationships reinforce the persons we are?
3. Name some ways that we can form our conscience in a positive or negative way.

Going Deeper: Can you think of a way you were reinforced by your family in a positive or negative way?[36]

Moral Beings

What does it mean to be a moral being? To be human is to be a moral being. It is to have inborn standards of conscience that guide our thinking and acting toward what is good and right over what is wrong. When we say a person is moral, it means that the person exhibits goodness in his or her free actions. One current ethicist wrote:

> *"Moral good is that which fosters human being and being more, human living and living more fully. It is the*

---
35 James Keating, *Spousal Prayer* (Omaha, Nebraska: IPF Publications, 2013), 38.
36 For those who come from a negative family background, make sure you assess your own situation in an honest way. Some past experiences require professional attention like counseling or therapy. In whatever form that may take, mistakes from our past can have an impact on our identity, self-worth, and relationships with others and with God.

> *ever-increasing growth in one's possibilities as a human person. Moral evil is that which puts limits on human beings and contracts human life."*[37]

In other words, choosing the moral good **expands** your life and your heart, bringing joy, peace, and fulfillment. Choosing moral evil, rather, **contracts** your life, making the heart heavy, extinguishing the joy.

The crisis of authentic love—the inability to put another's needs before one's own—cannot be underestimated. It is a moral crisis. The "new morality" of today seems to have also forced upon us a new ethical slogan: "Love alone is the standard for all morality." Sounds very attractive, but it comes with clear deficiencies.

> *Because human love is imperfect and "conflicting loves make conflicting claims on us, we must wrestle with moral problems. We are forced to seek a standard for making moral judgements and this seeking is the beginning of ethics for human behavior. To say "follow love" is not an ethics at all but a refusal to take ethical problems seriously. For those of us whose love is imperfect, the advice to follow love amounts to saying, "Do whatever you please"! In the end, to do what one pleases is to do what one pleases. It is not an ethical position.... It is moral chaos."*[38]

We human beings are free to choose. The truth is that we *do* have a choice in the matter. Submitting to our passions in a given moment, at the expense of what our reason indicates is good for us, can lead us down a painful road. Just think of the countless unwanted pregnancies in our world, and the unnecessary

---
37 Grisez and Shaw, *Beyond the New Morality*, 87.
38 Ibid., 109.

pain, despair, and even death that such a reality can bring to human life. Morality is about free choices, and choices make us either better or worse people. Furthermore, the great Christian thinkers of the past saw in the practice of making good moral choices the *perfectibility* of the person.[39] We literally perfect ourselves by our good choices. This is not some sort of self-creation or the inventing of what is important and not important to us.

There have been certain standards of human behavior that have always guided communities of people—call them the Ten Commandments or whatever you like. The fact is that every culture since the beginning of time has had such standards that have served as worthy guidelines for human flourishing. Even the early Christians knew the power of good choices: "Let us not grow weary of doing the good, for in due time we shall reap our harvest, if we do not give up"(Galatians 6:9).

Love as self-gift is *the one choice* that perfects us the most. In fact, St. John Paul II would argue that there is a law of love inside each of us that he called the *personalistic norm*: a human being is the kind of good who is incompatible to using; a person is that kind of good for whom the only proper response is love.[40] Love is the only proper response because we are more than just *something*. We are *someone*.

In the twenty-first century, living in the new pagan Rome, what are we to do? Over and over again we hear in the Gospel, "Be not afraid!" Believe in the power of the daily choice to love as a gift of yourself! This schooling in love is the integration of the

---

39 Aquinas, *Summa Theologica*, I–II, q. 28, a.5: "Love of a suitable good perfects and betters the lover; but love of a good which is unsuitable to the lover, wounds and worsens him. Wherefore man is perfected and bettered chiefly by the love of God; but is wounded and worsened by the love of sin."

40 Cfr. Wojtyla, *Love and Responsibility*, 41.

head and the heart. Such consistent choosing of the good of the other, over our own selfish ways, brings peace and fulfillment to both our relationships and to ourselves. Emotionally chaste living takes a well-formed moral compass to live.

Small Group Questions:
1. What does it mean to be a moral being?
2. What results in choosing the moral good? What results in choosing the moral evil?
3. Explain the concept of the perfectibility of the human person.

Human Sexuality

We end this chapter with a reflection on human sexuality. It is much more than just physical acts, but communicates a great mystery. The *invisible* mystery of God's interpersonal love has become *visible* in the physical human world, for us to see concretely through the human body. It is as if God were saying, "If you really want to know me, I who am, then look at my human creation. The physical design of male and female—both are made in my image and express characteristics of me." The male sex expresses strength, initiative, and protection. The female sex expresses receptivity, tenderness, and nurturing. St. John Paul II taught that when male and female come together, the giving and receiving language of self-gift love is imprinted into the very biology of male and female.

Our male to female body-person experience speaks of *being gift* to the other. The one-flesh union of male and female (Genesis 1:27) signifies precisely this: the man giving all that he is as a gift to the woman and the woman opening herself to receive the gift of the man. God so designed our bodies that this physical act of human love speaks of a total self-giving. And this act reflects who HE is: the source and essence of self-gift love. St. John Paul II calls this the spousal language of the body. One commentator on the works of St. John Paul II writes:

"The physical union is meant to express a *personal* union. Sexual intimacy is an expression of total love, total trust, total commitment. In giving their bodies to each other, couples are giving their very selves to each other."[41]

Our deepest reason for being human, for even existing, then, is to be a gift to another. Love as a total gift of self (self-gift) is truly our higher purpose. The very physicality of our human make-up is a manifestation of this. Mother Nature's design is hard to ignore even if we dismiss God's plan for sexuality. The bodies of two men, for example, are not designed to receive each other in a sexual way. The two do not fit together. "Even if people have such attractions, their bodies remain heterosexual: physically oriented towards the other (hetero) sex.[42] God's purpose for the sexual act is to be life-giving: babies and bonding. Be it the acts of same sex love or contraceptive heterosexual love, both are a disorder of God's purpose." Relationships with the wrong intention (selfishness, lust, cheating, adultery) are harmful and bring about a sort of spiritual illness and even death.

Love does not equal sex, and the word "sex" is not just about the act itself. Like love, it is much more. Today most people wrongly misunderstand and reduce the word *sex* or *sexual* to mean only one thing: *genital behavior*; in other words, they reduce masculinity and femininity to one physical act. This is

---

41 Edward Sri, *Love Unveiled* (San Francisco: Ignatius Press, 2015), 251.
42 Jason Evert, *Pure Manhood* (Scottsdale, AZ: Totus Tuus Press, 2018), 30-31. See end note no. 12 on HIV/AIDS disease impact.

incorrect. After speaking to hundreds of young adults, I learned how important it is to teach that our sexuality is not so much *what we do* as it is *who we are*. The fact is that we express our sexual identity in the way we walk, talk, dress, work, and recreate. Both man and woman are wholly sexual: body, mind, and spirit. Every one of us—whether married, those consecrated to God in celibacy, the sick, the old, and even children—are created as sexual persons with the calling to be bodily love-giving, and life-giving in countless and appropriate ways. Sexuality is our human capacity as whole persons to enter into love-giving, life-giving union, in and through the body, and this does not require any genital expression.[43]

This human capacity to share our very selves pervades our whole life and is not limited to bodily organs or genital activity.[44] In other words, everything is not just about the sex act. One can love another person in a non-physical way, without any intention of physical intimacy. This is true even when the physical capacity to do so is no longer possible. For example, if one of the spouses in a marriage loses the capacity to engage in physical intimacy, does this mean there is no love? The notion of sharing our very selves with another person places the value of the person *ahead* of their physical qualities. This thinking is totally countercultural to the "hookup" culture that defines people exclusively by their bodies and leaves people empty, alone, and sad.

Today, more often than not, human sexuality is reduced to the physical—how we function or our physical appearance. St. John Paul II says that the human body can never be reduced to mere

---

43 Sri, *Love Unveiled*, 95-98.
44 Cfr. Prokes, *Toward a Theology of the Body*, 95-96.

matter: it is a spiritualized body.⁴⁵ The person is a union of body and spirit.

Human beings stand alone in all creation as the only beings created as a union of the material and immaterial, body and spirit. We are body-persons. Our dignity comes from the whole package as physical *and* spiritual persons, not just the physical. The dignity of man or woman goes well beyond specific physical qualities, such as the color of the eyes or the shape of the body. Let's take a moment to see just how important the human body is. As one author aptly described it:

> *Our bodies are integral manifestation of who we are as human beings. Our bodies are not something we have, but something we are. The popular sense is that the self is contained within the body, but the truth is that we are our bodies. If our human dignity flows from being made in the image of God and therefore we are good, then our bodies are therefore good. To ignore or avoid our bodies is to avoid something of God.⁴⁶*

Human sexuality is ultimately the power of sharing oneself. It is *human,* and not identical to the animalistic drive found in subhuman species. We humans can share our very selves with another. Only humans can be sexual in this manner. Genuine love is the *giving and receiving* of self, not the *taking and getting* through physical strength or emotional manipulation.

If our higher purpose is to love, then the human-body-experience of love communicates something much more than the merely physical. We need to avoid reducing human love to something less than it is. We do this first by never reducing a

---
45   St. John Paul II, *Letter to Families* (Boston: Pauline Books and Media, 1994), 19.
46   Greg Bottaro, *Catholic Mindfulness* (North Palm Beach: Wellspring, 2018), 49-51.

person to merely his or her physical sexuality. Love is about the whole person: body and spirit!

Small Group Questions:
1. How does our human sexuality communicate a great mystery?
2. What does the word "sex" today often get reduced to? What is its' true meaning?

Going Deeper: Discuss how the moral principle of self-gift love can be derived from the physical design of the male and female bodies. While honoring everyone's need for love, how does one best respond to those with same sex attraction?[47]

---

[47] See the documentary called *The Third Way*. It offers an honest confession on how many have erred on the side of demonizing and alienating those with same sex attraction, rather than recognizing their human needs. It reflects well the teaching logic of the Gospel of "hate the sin, love the sinner" and offers concrete ways to heal the breach.

NOTES

CHAPTER THREE: OUR EMOTIONAL WORLD

This chapter is dedicated to understanding the emotional world within the human person, especially within the realm of human love. Our emotional world holds an integral place in who we are and how we love. These emotional "motors" of our inner world are spontaneous and involuntary. They are not positive or negative, but neutral. Understanding what they are and how to process them intelligently helps us grow in self-awareness, particularly with emotions like anger and shame. This chapter also distinguishes certain common notions like the "heart" from our emotional world. It also explores the paradox of accepting willingly the reality of suffering in love.

The Place of Emotions in the Human Person

As said earlier, emotions are the psychic movements within the human person which produce motion and energy to help us in life. They can be called motors because they cause us to move. Rather than bodily feelings like pain and hunger, here we are referring to the emotions that are reactions to stimuli from the world around us, like fear or hatred when we perceive evil, and love and joy when we perceive the good.[48] They are a response to whatever information our senses provide concerning the goodness, lack of goodness, usefulness, or harmfulness that things have for us.[49] Our emotions are part of our human existence through which man senses the good and perceives evil.

Different kinds of emotions move us to exert real effort. We need these motors because they motivate us to do more difficult

---
48 Baars, *Feeling and Healing Your Emotions*, 12-13.
49 Ibid., 12.

things, like studying for an exam so that we can do well in school or exercising to keep our bodies healthy. Emotions push us to move, react, and do what is needed, to achieve what we desire.

Our emotions are God-given and are meant to enrich our life, particularly in how we love. Self-gift love implies a giving of our whole self to another, which naturally includes our emotional world. Our emotions are like "sensors." They help our reason detect things that are important to us. To love merely from our intelligence (the head), and not include our emotions, can be hazardous, even dangerous, resulting in a love that is incomplete. We do not have emotions for things that we do not care about. The lesson here is to pay attention to your emotions. To authentically love with our whole selves *does* require the healthy contribution of our emotions!

For centuries, this point was taught by some of the greatest and wisest of people. The philosopher Thomas Aquinas showed that our emotions should not be ignored, but are important in our seeking the good especially, if that Good is God.[50] "We experience *delight* in God's word, *compassion* for our neighbor, *sorrow* for sin, *hunger* for justice, and *joy* in his presence—all vitally part of our loving God and others" (Mark 12:30).[51] This is why Christ called us to love with all our heart, all our soul, and all our mind.

Jesus, the great model, shows us the way. In the Gospel, for example, we see Christ weeping before the death of his friend Lazarus. Even though Jesus knows he will raise Lazarus up from the dead in a matter of minutes, the reality of death, something so contrary to the good of human life, moves Jesus to cry for his friend. "He wept" (John 17:35). He is fully human and allows

---

50 St. Thomas Aquinas, *The Summa Theologica*, I-II, q. 59, a.5.
51 Art and Larraine Bennett, *The Emotions God Gave You* (Frederick, MD: Word among Us Press, 2011), 18.

the emotion of grief to surface as a normal human response to experience of sorrow for someone he loves. We call this healthy emotional integration.

Emotional chastity (loving with your head and heart) guides the maturing process of emotional integration and becomes critical to one's way of life. The purpose of our emotional world is to help each of us love in an ever more perfect and uniquely human way.

Small Group Questions:
1. How are our emotions like a motor? Why is this a good thing?
2. Do we need our emotional world to love with our whole selves?

Emotions: What Do I Do with Them?[52]

Because our *impulsive* emotional reactions can get us into trouble, we often believe that emotions are bad and hinder us in life. Consider a comment made to me by a young girl, "Maybe I am too emotional for a man to love me." The power of our emotional world may seem to take away our freedom due to its intensity, even to the point that we do not know what to do with such feelings. We feel powerless. We may think that this intense moment is never going to end.

These strong emotions can spin in our hearts' emotive responses of false and unworthy love towards ourselves, others, and even God. In many faith circles, for example, negative emotions often translate into "I am not a good person." NO! The integration of our emotional world begins by understanding

---

[52] Some of these reflections are taken from a talk given by Dr. Jonathan and Dr. Alex Marcotte on emotional integration at, the SLC Conference, January 1, 2020, Phoenix AZ.

that our emotions are part of who we are. But they do not control us. *They are not us.* We need to avoid labeling ourselves in unhealthy ways because of struggles with negative emotions.

Generally speaking, people today have poor skill in handling their emotions. Particularly in Western culture, with its tendency to seek immediate gratification, uncomfortable emotions can often be displaced through pleasure-seeking. We evade negative emotions by seeking gratification to numb how we feel. For example, I feel sad or lonely, and so I eat to "feel" better. I feel stressed after work, so I have many glasses of wine. This is an unhealthy way to deal with our emotions. We need to *feel the feeling,* not eat or drink it away.

Rather than sharing their emotions, some people shut down their emotions. The problem of sidestepping, or even worse, suppressing our emotions is that repression tends to shut down *all feelings*—the negative and the positive. The "stuffing" of our emotional world also takes up a lot of energy. It is exhausting. This constant management of our emotions keeps us from being able to freely say yes to so many amazing opportunities that life offers.

It is true that our emotions can react in milliseconds while our poor brains need time to catch up. However, if you train yourself to *pause, process, and reflect* before acting, then likely you will not be acting on mere impulse, or unrefined emotion. You will be able to refrain from emotionally charged behavior that might be hurtful toward yourself and others. The popular movement of "mindfulness" is all about this pause, process, and reflect.

By taking the following steps one can develop a healthy "presence of mind"[53]:

---

[53] These steps are an imperfect summary of some of the suggested exercises within the current

a. Take a few moments to sit in stillness. A few deep breaths help.
b. Next, name the emotion experienced.
c. Identify the triggers that might have caused the reaction.
d. Locate the physical place in your body where it surfaces and causes you unease. Acknowledge it, but do not judge it.
e. Discern the desires the emotion provokes. From where do they come? Are they good or bad, moral or immoral?
f. Finally, what is the most appropriate way to share it?

Developing a habitual application to this mindful process allows one to respond rather than simply react. Reacting is the blind motor (will) with no light (reason). It is more impulsive, more in the moment without any reflection. Responding, rather, involves both the light and the motor working together. It is a pausing. It is composure and reflection. The light of reason is fundamental to human maturity, and for a healthy and mature response in love involving the head and heart.

The two most important points are, first, that each of us is free to respond to our emotions or not, despite their intensity, and second, that emotions need to be shared and should not be suppressed. It is the way we freely *choose to share* our emotions that makes a human action good or bad, just or unjust. We are not powerless over our emotions. Human beings *can* respond and not just react. What you *feel* is one thing; what you *do* is another. This is called self-possession.

In the arena of human love, we can respond to another person *as a person*, avoiding the often-regretted mistreatment of another. Clearly our passions need to be schooled and purified

---

mindfulness movement. They are meant only to give one an idea of how *pause, process, and reflect* might look like in action.

to form a love built on respect and kindness and not on fleeting impulses which can lead us to regret and sadness. Nonetheless, this "schooling" is not some kind of "dictatorship," as if our drives, feelings, and motivations slavishly follow will and intellect. Rather, it is a happy integration, and happiness is in the affective domain of the person.[54] This purification comes in the right ordering of our emotional world and is possible for each one of us.

Small Group Questions:

1. Why is it important to know that our emotions do not control us?
2. What are the repercussions of suppressing your emotions?
3. Discuss the mindful habit of *pause, process, and reflect*.

The Case of Anger

Anger is a good example of an emotion that is not easy to integrate into good decision making, which is the hallmark of emotional chastity. Anger is an intense emotional state that involves a strong uncomfortable and hostile response to a perceived hurt or threat. It is a tremendous emotional stimulant and it often comes with tremendous consequences. It is worth asking ourselves, "Is there ever a case for anger?"

Uncontrolled anger leaves its negative mark in so many aspects of life: slander, domestic abuse, rape, and many others. However, not all anger is negative. Anger can be the emotion that

---

[54] Dietrich von Hildebrand, *The Heart* (South Bend, IN: St. Augustine's Press, 2007), 4. This dense yet wonderful book seeks to integrate the domain of human emotion within the larger perspective of human experience (spiritual, intellectual, volitional, moral), allowing for a deeper integration in the human person.

fuels one to overcome great obstacles, like fighting injustice and evil. One current example of this would be MADD (Mothers Against Drunk Driving), and the great work they have done to bring awareness to this terrible social problem. Justified anger set on the right course by both reason (head) and love (heart) can be a catalyst for inspiring us to serve others. Despite anger's emotional intensity, we still have freedom of choice. We have the capacity to use that energy in a positive, not negative, way.

The alternative to giving in to an emotion such as anger is simply suppressing it. It is acting as if what we feel is bad, unimportant, or not to be trusted. It is common knowledge in the world of psychology that the consequences of suppressed emotions will eventually appear in all sorts of negative ways. This creates an emotive climate that does not allow for proper emotional development, and hence healthy maturity, in the person. An example of the consequences of suppressed anger is the ever-more frequent cases of abuse, which violates the dignity of the other person. Anger is a natural response of the abused toward the abuse. Honest recognition of what has happened is of crucial importance for both sides. For the abused person, a healthy response to such harm would be, "This was an offense, this was extremely hurtful and unfair, and I'm angry that it happened." Such a response is well exemplified by the words of St. Paul: "Be angry, but sin not" (Ephesians 4:26). The early Christian apostle is saying: "Go ahead and *feel* your anger because it is natural to feel that way when someone or something hurts you. Recognize and be aware of that emotion. Do not repress it. However, beware of what you *do* with it, because the wrong choice could be hurting you, others, and God."

So much of today's healing ministry takes people back to painful memories where emotions were either suppressed or indulged, helping them undo those emotional "knots." The *naming and owning* of past emotions help people move on in life, particularly from broken relationships. This form of therapeutic reflection unlocks serious healing power and is a healthy way to grow in emotional maturity: knowing yourself and avoiding dependence on strong emotions like anger. In the end, good therapy is about helping to remove barriers so one can love. The habit of emotional chastity frees one from the enslavement of unhealthy emotions, thus enabling one to love another completely.

Our emotions, including anger, are an essential part of who we are. We can develop self-dominion over even a volatile emotion such as anger. When properly directed, our emotions can be a huge impetus for the good, and often help us to accomplish feats beyond our sheer willpower. The bottom line is, our emotions are not "leaders," but "followers." It is the light of reason that leads our emotions to their best and most fruitful end.

Small Group Questions:

1. When can the emotion of anger be good?
2. Is it good to suppress our anger? Why or why not?
3. How does the light of reason help us to best use our anger?

The Uniqueness of Shame

Shame is another emotion that can help us better understand the human person and love. Only human beings feel shame. St. John Paul II says that shame is bound up with the nature of the human person and is a clear manifestation of our personhood. In the ambit of human love, it is the one emotion that functions to help us exclude or reject an attitude of using another person in our behavior.[55]

---
55 Wojtyla, *Love and Responsibility*, 175.

There is good shame and bad shame. As one psychologist said, good shame is that normal emotion that "gives us permission to be human by telling us of our limits and by keeping us in our human boundaries."[56] In other words, we could call it our "dignity-meter." We know that we are special and deserve special behavior, and when we act against that dignity or are treated by another in an undignified way, then the shame button is pushed.[57] There is also bad shame, which can translate into "I am bad" and causes us to question our essential goodness. For example, many women have shared with me their sexual promiscuity before marriage and many men have shared with me their pornography addictions. They can often feel like bad people because of it. These freely chosen actions do hurt the person in question; however, it does not mean that they are fundamentally bad people. Bad shame is the inability to let go of guilt of the past, forgive oneself, and live in the present.

Shame can cause certain natural physiological changes in us, like turning red in the face when we are embarrassed or ashamed. This reaction can happen when things go bad or when things go well. For example, when we are caught lying, we feel shame; or when our good deeds are recognized, we may feel shame. What is common to both responses is that shame arises when something is meant to stay private, but nevertheless becomes public. It seems to express the inviolability of each person and forbids the abuse of that purity, toward oneself or toward another. This human experience is certainly seen when it comes to sexual shame.

St. John Paul II's profound reflection on the book of Genesis regarding the creation of man, and then his "fall from innocence," reveals the nature of sexual shame. The words "I was afraid,

---

56 John Bradshaw, *Healing Shame That Binds You* (Deerfield, FL: Health Communications Inc. 1988), vii.
57 Wojtyla, *Love and Responsibility*, 179. "The value of the person is closely connected with its inviolability, its status as something more than just an object of use."

because I was naked" (Genesis 3:10) reveal a break in the original spiritual and physical unity of man. The original harmony inside man and with those around him is disturbed due to sin. Something within the body is now at war with the spirit. "The unity of the person is threatened. This is especially true with lust. The "person of lust" does not control their body with ease and naturalness, as the man of original innocence, before sin, did. Self-mastery is essential to the moral integrity of human beings. Lust attacks the person at his core by throwing body and spirit out of balance."[58]

One of the least discussed aspects of today's sexualized culture is its tendency to cause shame in people. Sexual arousal naturally feels good in the moment, yet disordered sexual intimacy with self or another can lead to shameful emotions. Disordered sexual intimacy does not produce the communion people are seeking, either with one another, with self, or with God. This can happen inside or outside marriage. Research in the social sciences increasingly shows that these types of behavior can cause:

> *"guilt, regret, temporary self-loathing, rumination, diminished self-esteem, a sense of having used someone else or been used, a sense of having let yourself down, discomfort about having to lie or conceal sex from family, anxiety over the depth and course of the relationship, and concern over the place or role of sex in the relationship."*[59]

In other words, human beings, in their deepest consciousness, do not want to be treated this way and yet do not seem to understand the harm caused to themselves or caused to others when participating in this disordered behavior.

---

[58] William May, *The Scriptures, Human sexuality and Sexual Morality, and Pope John Paul II's "Theology of the Body"*, retrieved June 8, 2005 from http://christendom-awake.org/pages/may/scriptures.htm.

[59] Mark Regnerus and Jeremy Uecker, *Premarital Sex in America: How Young Americans Meet, Mate, and Think About Marrying*, as quoted in the National Catholic Register, January 25, 2014, Marion Crowe, *Chastity: The Forgotten Virtue*.

Even though some may try to dismiss this "gut feeling" of shame as scrupulosity or mere religious guilt, shameful feelings are like the light on the car's dashboard blinking when something is not quite right with the car. Sexual shame is that blinking light in us, part of the wiring of the human person, and its resounding power in us is meant to prompt us to ask, "Are we hurting ourselves and others?"

It is important to mention a key distinction between guilt and shame. "Guilt is adaptive and helpful—it's holding something we've done or failed to do up against our values and feeling psychological discomfort. Shame, on the other hand, is the intensely painful feeling or experience of believing that we are flawed and therefore unworthy of love and belonging— something we've experienced, done, or failed to do makes us unworthy of connection."[60] Guilt is "I did something wrong/bad" and shame is "I am bad." Either way, in contrast, healthy and respectful love towards oneself and another person affirms and validates a person's fundamental dignity and sacredness.

Small Group Questions:

1. Distinguish good shame from bad shame.
2. Talk about the nature of sexual shame in the light of the book of Genesis.
3. How are shameful feelings like the light on the car's dashboard?

Going Deeper: Name some experiences of where the guilt of "doing bad" can quickly lead to believing "I am bad."

---

60 Brené Brown, *Shame v. Guilt*, January 14, 2013. https://brenebrown.com/blog/2013/01/14/shame-v-guilt.

Emotions and the Heart

So often today the word "heart" seems to express just a bunch of emotional impulses. Movies, books, and songs urge people to "follow your heart" like it should be the final decision-maker. Yet our emotional world and the heart are not the same things. With "the heart," we mean something different from emotionalism or sentimentality.

The heart could be defined as the interior "headquarters" of the person, the dwelling place where I am, where I live. "It is the living union of blood and spirit that characterizes man; the source of his becoming, and by conversion, re-becoming."[61] It directs appropriate emotional responses such as "joy at seeing something beautiful, sadness at tragedy, etc., as opposed to inappropriate responses such as hardness of heart, or overanalyzing experiences."[62]

The heart includes all the weakness and all the strength of the human person. Since, as human beings, we are often a mystery even unto ourselves, the wisdom of the Scriptures cautions us about the impulsive dissent of the heart: "The heart is deceitful above all things and is exceedingly corrupt. Who can know it?" (Jeremiah 17:9) or "Keep your heart with all vigilance, for from it flow the springs of life" (Proverbs 4:23).

We need to honestly pause on the movements of our heart: the inner restlessness that agitates us. Slow down, ask advice from a trusted friend, spend time hearing ourselves think, make time for quiet prayer. It is worth it. One of the key principles for making good choices is to *never act* when you find yourself in a moment of interior desolation or angst. Rather, stay the course,

---
61 Romano Guardini, *The Last Things* (New York: Pantheon Books, 1951), 75.
62 Dietrich Von Hildebrand, *The Heart* (South Bend, IN: St. Augustine's Press, 2012), 78.

and be firm and constant in your current resolution, no matter how unpleasant it might be.[63] How many of us would gladly like to take back that rash email or text message we sent in a moment of impulsive annoyance at another person only to have it come back and shame us? Pressing the pause button allows the heart to connect with the head.

It is precisely this thoughtful pausing before the movements of the heart that refines our thinking and brings a sense of balance to our lives. Emotional chastity helps precisely in this harmonizing process. It purifies the inner eye of the heart, so to speak, so the heart may stay consistent with its life compass. For example, when a young man seeks to build a friendship with a special girl, rather than follow his lustful tendencies encouraging him to seduce her, it is the head and the heart *together* that direct the young man to the truth: "She is worth my self-control." Or, when a young woman is discerning a decision of great consequence—to consecrate her life exclusively to God and give up the prospect of marriage and family—and is faced with many conflicting emotions, it is both her head and her heart that agree to the truth: "God deserves that I at least try," displacing the paralyzing fear of "What if I am mistaken or will this decision really satisfy me?" Emotional chastity creates the inner climate of mindfulness that obliges us to honesty, truthfulness, and fairness towards God, oneself, and one's fellow man.

Perhaps this essential harmonizing of the whole person is what we mean by purity of heart. "Blessed are the pure in heart, for they shall see God" (Matthew 5:8). When the heart and head are synchronized, we see in a pure, whole, new way. Pope Benedict XVI says that "when the whole person is harmonized, we can even see the Divine. We are capable of perceiving God and

---

[63] See Rule #5 of discernment in the Spiritual Exercises of St. Ignatius of Loyola.

the presence of God in others."[64] Purity of heart is the total ordering of the person in love. This is the hope that God has for all of us.

Small Group Questions:
1. How are emotions and "the heart" different?
2. Why do we need to pause when our heart is restless and agitated?

Going Deeper: Name some experiences that reflect the importance of harmonizing the head and the heart, and the balance it brings into our lives?

Heart-Intuition

In his writing on human love, St. John Paul II refers to a type of heart-intuition each of us has. He describes it as an *echo*[65]: the heart resonance of the original beginning when man and woman were first created before selfish love (sin) had entered the world. The echo is that experience of original unity when perfect intimacy between God and between persons was complete. The head and the heart are in perfect unison when a true knowing of the goodness of the other, and a pure desire to honor it, exist between two persons.

However, once sin entered the world of relationships, we became estranged from God and at odds to that interior calling to be true to love as a total self-gift.

> *"As a break with God, the first sin had for its first consequence the rupture of the original communion between*

---

64 Pope Benedict XVI, *Jesus of Nazareth* (New York: Doubleday, 2007), 92-93.
65 St. John Paul II, *Theology of the Body* (Boston: Pauline News and Media, 2006), 55, 4.

> *man and woman. Their relations were distorted by mutual recriminations; their mutual attraction, the Creator's own gift, changed into a relationship of domination and lust."*[66]

Sin has almost silenced the echo, but it has not completely silenced it. The yearning of the heart continues. We sense that we are incomplete, no matter how much we try to fill that void with stuff. We are in search of another to make "sense" of ourselves. We are created for bliss, for ecstasy, and our hearts know it.[67] It's like the heart knows what love should look and feel like. Our very humanity is wired for it.

It seems that only when we experience genuine love, in and around us, that we begin to hear again the faint echo of the original calling within us. In other words, only if we see it, feel it, and practically touch it, does it stir in us that slumbering heart-intuition of a renewed belief that such love *does* exists. When relationships are centered on authentic love as self-gift, they build us up, affirm us, and inspire us to want the same for our own lives. Truly it is a Divine stirring in our heart of hearts for perfect love that only God awakens and, in the end, fills.

To illustrate such a power, I remember the story of a young man who rented a room from a family of six while in college. This family's faith life was front and center, and he was at best skeptical when it came to faith. Nonetheless, within a relatively short period of time, after witnessing, and more importantly, experiencing the love in this family, he began asking questions and connecting their behavior with what they believed. Their forgiveness and patience with each other, though imperfect, spoke to him in a powerful way. He wanted for himself what

---
66   CCC 1607.
67   Christopher West, *Fill These Hearts* (New York: Image Books, 2012), Chapter 1.

they had. Over time, he became a young man hungry to know God and his ways, to the point of wanting to give up everything and consecrate his life to God. He is a seminarian today. This all started from witnessing authentic love within this family.

It is true that within a humanity so prone to selfishness, we do not see and experience such love very often. We can lose faith that it even exists. Yet our hearts, in the end, *do* know. Human beings need to see selfless love, literally incarnated in others, to aspire to the same. This is the fundamental crisis of our culture. We go for the counterfeit, for what appears to be true love, and it disappoints us every time. This truth is so fundamental that it challenges us to make a sober *head and heart* examination of the relationships in our lives. Are they truly life- giving or death-dealing, and for what part am I responsible?

Small Group Questions:
1. Why is the heart intuition like an "echo" in the human person?
2. What has sin done to that "echo"?
3. What type of experiences awaken in us the echo of the heart?

Love Doesn't Always "Feel" Good

Here we enter into the paradox of that interior echo for authentic love that is placed in us by God. It is called suffering. We equate the word "love" today with everything *but* suffering. Love is something so exhilarating, so adrenaline-charged, it could never involve pain. However, the "yes" to love *is* a source of pain and suffering, because love always requires the letting go of the "selfish me," in which I allow myself to be pruned and wounded. Love cannot exist without this painful renunciation of myself."[68] This principle holds true in every state of life.

Take the story of the consecrated sister of Mother Teresa's community, who every day bathed a homeless man. This man did not believe in God and would often blaspheme God to her face. One day he spit on her because he was so enraged that she would not respond to his rants. She stopped what she was doing rather than aggravate the situation, and she left. The next day, she returned as if nothing happened and continued to bathe him as she always did. He broke down crying and begged her forgiveness. The words, "truly I tell you, just as you did not do it to one of the least of these, you did not do it to me" (Matthew 25:45) had so convicted her that she chose to manage her interior emotions (anger, resentment, spite) and respond in love to his severe words. Perhaps the invalid man had never experienced unconditional love in his life, but rather only pain and selfishness.

This is what the early Christians called "foolishness" (1 Corinthians 1:18-19). It was their capacity to follow the example of Jesus's own love, to bear the suffering out of love in all things, even when everything seemed to be against them, be it their own rebellious selves or even death! This is why, for example, to this very day the Christian martyrs "continue to arouse such interest, to draw agreement, to win such a hearing and to invite emulation. The martyrs provide evidence of a love that has no need of lengthy arguments in order to convince. The martyrs stir in us a profound trust because they give voice to what we already feel and they declare what we would like to have the strength to express."[69] They have found the truth about life and love in the encounter with Christ, and nothing and no one could

---

68 Pope Benedict XVI, *Saved by Hope* (San Francisco: Ignatius Press, 2008), 38.
69 St. John Paul II, *Fides et Ratio* (Boston: Pauline Books and Media, 1998), 45.

ever change this. Their attitude teaches us that in all love, human or Divine, there is nothing lost through sacrifice.

Of course, this is ultimately fulfilled in the example of Christ himself. He was a man fully alive in his total gift of self: "I lay down my life in order to take it up again. No one takes it from me, but I lay it down of my own accord. I have power to lay it down, and I have power to take it up again" (John 10:17-18). This love is transformative. It restores value and meaning where and when it has been lost. Something is always being re-created, something apparently lost being found.

The married state is also abundantly filled with opportunities for purification and thus a "re-creation" or "re-discovery" of sorts. Expecting and embracing sacrifice when it comes our way is key to a fruitful marriage because it is living in the reality of human imperfection. For example, I know of a married couple who gradually grew apart. The husband was working too much, and the wife was too busy with their children. They were not nurturing their relationship. He slowly began giving more time to his social work circles after hours, which led him to visit all sorts of seedy places. Then he started going on his own to the same places. She, sensing his distance and feeling used only for one thing, began to reject him more and more, which continued to drive him away. Finally, he confessed his deeds to his wife, and after much pain and many tears, she also owned up to her selfish behavior. They began to work together, resulting in a rebirth of their marriage. Embracing and working through heavy affliction can bring a special fruitfulness to a marriage.

Yet sadly, how often today are we bombarded with, and even succumb to, the opposite message in social media, that everything is just perfect: the carefree couple with ample amounts of disposal free time and money to travel, always having fun. Any couples with a little sense know that this is truly "fake news."

To think that one can taste this life-giving love while escaping the unspoken reality of sacrifice is pure delusion. The gymnasium of authentic human love *is* sacrifice. The daily grind of learning to love patiently imperfect people, despite the natural lack of gusto to do so, is, in fact, love. It is not always pretty nor picture-perfect. When we are courageous enough to embrace it, then such love rouses the heart to new heights of love, and the impact is profound. Even the most hardened of hearts are attracted, moved, and at times melted by such an example, by deeds of sheer goodness and burning love.

Small Group Questions:
1. How can suffering and love go together?
2. What do the Christian martyrs teach us about love?
3. Why is sacrifice the "gymnasium" of authentic human love?

NOTES

CHAPTER FOUR: PROGRESSION OF LOVE

How do we arrive to this kind of deeper, more mature love for another person? Love as total gift of self is not automatic. It takes an intentional choice. Both the head and heart must work together to bring about this kind of love.

The progress of human love depends on each person's free choice. Love can progress and mature to be a total gift of self *if it is based on the good of the other*; otherwise, it will stagnate. The great TV personality of the 1950s, Fulton Sheen, explained this process of maturing love:

> "Love is like a seed that is planted, which grows with constant and daily care, renews itself amidst storms and winds, rejoices in its blossoms, thrills to its fruits, dies to itself in winter of its discontent and arises again in the freshness of a higher life in the Easter of its glory. Love must undergo a continuous transformation, under penalty of sinking otherwise into dullness and monotony."[70]

In other words, there are laws of growth. To move love from its merely sensual early stages to a deeper gift of self, self-sacrifice is the price that we need to expect and embrace. Embracing the cost and expense of love for the other helps one avoid seeing the other as a mere burden or a roadblock to one's own happiness.

Emotional chastity nurtures a healthy maturing of love centered on the dignity of the other person. It is a channeling of our positive dispositions, the moderation of our selfish tendencies, and the steady improving of our personal efforts to express unselfish love in thought, word, and deed. As one learns to

---
70 Sheen, *Being Human*, 109.

practice an ever-maturing love that demands "all of me" over what more naturally appeals to us, the steps of growth are marked by imperfection and failure. Forming any good habit takes time and a lot of effort. But over time, our possessive selfish tendencies become less dominant as life tutors us with opportunities to grow and experience joy in giving and receiving love. The effort to love another person in this way unlocks the amazing potential inherent in every human being. St. John Paul II assures us that "we are most fully actualized through sacrificial love for another."[71]

St. John Paul II breaks down the evolution of human love into four stages: (1) attraction, (2) desire, (3) good will, and (4) unconditional.[72] He is describing here the particular love between a man and a woman.

Small Group Questions:
1. Why does love have laws of growth?
2. What role does emotional chastity have in this maturing process?

First Stage: Love as Attraction

Attraction-love is the first stage of human love. St. John Paul II calls it the "raw material" of love. In this stage, our emotions are moved and attracted to something good about this other someone. This particular good of the other is based in the sensual values of the person: nice smile, good sense of humor, beautiful eyes. Attraction-love is like fondness; it takes a liking to the other. It is of the senses and the sentiments and is the first and natural stage of a budding human love.

---
71 Wojtyla, *Love and Responsibility*, 82.
72 Cfr. Wojtyla, *Love and Responsibility*, 74-95.

Nonetheless, attraction-love is not necessarily romantic. We can be attracted or fond of a lot of different things and have no romantic sentiments. For example, a teacher can be fond of her student and his intellectual capacities, or you can connect with a neighbor who happens to like your baseball team. It is a sensitivity toward certain properties or characteristics of the other person with which you connect. In this stage, the person is simply saying "I like this or that about this person." It is an ability to react to a certain good one finds in the other person.

Even in this early stage of attraction-love, however, St. John Paul II says there is some hint of "I want," and therefore the danger exists of having a "use-attitude." For example, men are naturally drawn to beauty and most are moved by the power of physical beauty. This is normal and healthy. In a sense, physical beauty can just "hit" a person. Yet "in a consumerist society, the sense of beauty is impoverished, and consequently joy fades. Everything is there to be purchased, possessed, or consumed, including people."[73]

Yet the physical attraction a person may feel towards the beauty of another is not necessarily the truth of the whole person, but only a partial value. There is also the inner beauty of the person. We know that women, for example, are more than their physical beauty. They have an important personal history, experience, and intelligence that makes them who they are beyond the physical. Self-gift love includes the beauty of the inner and outer person, all of the person. It is not a love between mere *physical bodies* but rather *persons*.[74]

Nevertheless, today we see the dominance of a mentality centered on what a person is on the outside (physical) over what they are inside (spiritual). This mentality is reflected in the popular

---
[73] Pope Francis, *Amoris Laetitia* (New York: Beacon Publishing), 127.
[74] Cfr. Wojtyla, *Love and Responsibility*, 78-79.

song by Ed Sheeran's "Shape of You" and the constant cry "I am in love with your body." Attraction-love may draw us to something particularly characteristic of the other, but that quality that we are attracted to is attached to *a person*, and the whole of this person deserves to be respected. The pornographic culture prevalent today promotes the body over the person. "From St. John Paul's perspective, the problem with pornography is not that it reveals too much of a person but that it reveals too little."[75]

It is precisely in this early stage of love when our emotional-affective reactions to the qualities of another can distort one's perception of the truth of the person. St. John Paul II says that our emotions do not generally possess an intellectual *power*; that is, they are not concerned about knowing the whole truth of the other person. It is here the old saying rings true, "love is blind." Attraction-love is not a helpful guide in seeing the truth of the other, so to speak, because it only sees partially.[76]

Obviously, this can be very dangerous for new love. Our emotions can falsify attraction, perceiving a value that might not even be present. Once the affective reaction towards those qualities pass away, often we are left disappointed, deprived of the good we thought we had found. How often do we hear of young people getting caught up with these crazy, selfish, and even abusive individuals? St. John Paul II says this is why such intense attraction can quite quickly turn to intense repulsion for the same person.[77] I have often observed this in my many conversations with young people. The person you once found so awesome can quickly become so enraging.

This attraction stage of love needs coaching from our reason about the truth of the whole person. Am I seeing this person for

---
75 Christopher West, *Good News About Sex and Marriage* (Cincinnati, OH: Servant Books, 2004), 86.
76 Wojtyla, *Love and Responsibility*, 77.
77 Ibid., 78.

what they are? Are others telling me things that should concern me? Emotional chastity promotes personal reflection, connecting the heart with the head so as to choose sensibly. Developing the habit of pausing and reflecting on experiences of intense attraction will help illuminate us to an important truth: the intensity of emotion is *not* a measurement of love. Rather, it is *the responsibility* that one feels for the other that indicates the measurement of love.[78] Am I willing to make sacrifices for the other in very specific ways, putting my needs and wants aside for what he or she may need? Is the other willing to do the same for me, or is it always a one-sided deal? Is the other actively finding out how to love me better?

St. John Paul II says that when the subjective truth of our emotions ("I feel this attraction to this person") and the objective truth of the value of this person ("This person is more than their good looks, or sexy body, or personality") are integrated and harmonious with each other, they give a special genuineness to the person.[79] Maturing that integration process is precisely the goal of emotional chastity.

Small Group Questions:
1. Discuss how attraction-love is the raw material of love.
2. Even though you may be attracted to someone's physical qualities, does this qualify as love? How does human freedom play a role here?
3. Why is it important that reason coach the emotional side of attraction-love?

Going Deeper: Is it normal for those who are already committed to a particular state in life, i.e., marriage or consecrated life, to be attracted to other people? Discuss this point.

---

78 It is important to note the opposite reality too, where very little emotion is felt. Just because you don't feel like you are in love doesn't mean you don't have the capacity or ability to love.
79 Cfr. Wojtyla, *Love and Responsibility*, 78.

Second Stage: Love as Desire

Desire is the second stage of human love. Although love is not merely attraction or desire, both attraction and desire are components of a love that is maturing, and both are essential to human love as a whole. Love as desire is going from "I like" (attraction) to "I want" (desire). It sees the good of the other and wants to possess it, to experience it. It says, "Wow that's good. I want that for myself".

According to St. John Paul II, it is in this stage where love is experienced as a longing for a person. It could be argued that this is the stage when we understand our incompleteness and that we are limited on our own. We simply desire more. Perhaps this is why love as desire, often referred to as erotic love, possesses a certain suggestion of Divine love. "As food is for the body, as body is for the soul, as the material is for the spiritual, so the flesh is for the eternal." That is why in the language of human love, we can often detect the language of divinity, such as "worship," "angel," or "adore." Love passes from an affection for outer appearances to those inner depths of personality which embody the Divine Spirit.[80] Yet desire-love is not an end in itself. It "is a bridge which one crosses, it is not meant to be a buttress where one sits and rests, it is not an airport but an airplane; it is always going somewhere else, upward and onward."[81] This stage of love presupposes incompleteness, deficiency, yearning for completion, and an attraction for enrichment.

God made men and women to need each other. Love as desire originates in a need and aims to find a good which it lacks.[82] It

---

80   Cfr. Sheen, *Being Human*, 108. St. John Paul II says that this love as desire is the starting point also for a person's relationship with God. Man needs God as does every other creature simply in order *to be*. See *Love and Responsibility*, 80.
81   Ibid.
82   Wojtyla, *Love and Responsibility*, 81.

communicates "I need another to complete me." Love as desire is the crystallization of the fact that men and women are objectively bound for each other. It is a longing for some good for its own sake and communicates, "I want you because you are a good for me." The common notion of *opposites attract* seems to be based on this. One party is disorganized, the other organized; one is friendly and outgoing, the other more reserved and quieter. This common experience can move the couple to say, "You are good for me." Be it a heterosexual or homosexual attraction, the same is true. This person fulfills a need I have. Since love as desire implies the filling of the other's needs, completing what is incomplete, great care needs to be given not to make this desire-love a reason for selfish personal ends expressed in "using" the other.

Certain dangers can appear in this stage. First, as St. John Paul II says, mere sensual desire can overshadow desire love and can thus deform the love between man and woman.[83] Desire can rob men and women of that deeper more fulfilling love that is discovered only as love matures, and it can mask forms of lust in the human heart. If we define the disorder of lust as more "taking" than "giving," the expression of lust will take different forms in men and women. Oftentimes for men it is expressed in a physical way, and for women it is expressed more emotionally. Lust is not always plain and obvious. Sometimes it is concealed, so that it masquerades as love.

For example, take the more concealed case of emotional lust. A young girl comes from a broken home life and seeks to have her emotional needs filled by her boyfriend. She feels "validated" whenever she spends time with him although the conversation is all about her and her family situation. One could say she is

---

83 This holds true for heterosexual or homosexual attraction. If I love this person then I will manage my physical or emotional attraction to them, putting his or her good before my own.

"using" him, albeit unconsciously, for that affirming love that should come first and foremost from a stable and loving home life. Perhaps she rationalizes it as okay because she is "giving" him what he wants: physical intimacy. At the same time, the boyfriend puts up with the constant drama of the problems in her family because she is available to him physically. Here the old adage seems to prove true: "Boys give love to get sex, and girls give sex to receive love." In the end, the two are using one another, "taking" what each one needs in the moment, with the desire for authentic love in second place.

The argument today is that there is nothing wrong with this situation. Both get what they want, so what's the problem? If love is just about what "I want," then this simply confirms the "if it feels good just do it" mentality, promoting immediate gratification and short-term happiness at the expense of another, knowingly or unknowingly. St. John Paul II says that the early "raw material of love," the sensual and emotional elements of both attraction-love and desire-love, creates states of feeling within persons and between persons that are *favorable* to love. However, it is still *not* love,[84] and if it grows out of nothing more than lust, the desire to use, it will not lead to love. On the contrary, it denies authentic love.

Because mere sensual desire impels people very powerfully toward physical intimacy, boundaries are important. What fosters self-esteem and self-reliance for the other person? How can we avoid the pitfalls of disrespect and manipulation while maintaining mutual respect for each other? **Boundaries**. The definition of *boundaries* is a "qualified no" that says what, where, when, and under what circumstances you will engage or not engage with the other person. Again, "you say no, not because you do not love him or her but because you do. You are forcing the

---
84 Cfr. Wojtyla, *Love and Responsibility*, 159.

other to intentionally state his or her purpose through actions, and detach from any unhealthy passion, because you love him or her. You are not responsible for making the other person obey the boundaries. You are responsible only for following the boundaries yourself and for reinforcing them."[85] Healthy boundaries gives the couple a "safe space" so that genuine love can develop in a spirit of mutual respect without introducing the complications of physical intimacy too soon.

Rather than look at boundaries as something negative or deficient, we have a unique gift as human beings to be able to consciously reflect before we react. Nonetheless, the culture has taken a truth about our emotional world—that it is something that spontaneously moves us, like being bumped around on a subway without choosing it —and turned into "it's outside our freedom to do anything about our emotions." This translates very quickly into "it's outside of our responsibility, even our conscience, to say no to following this attraction." It is important to know that *there is freedom to choose* at this stage of love, and therefore we are free to respond or not respond.

We know intuitively that if fleeting instinctual pleasure brought happiness, the world would sparkle like the sun, at least half the time. Yet, when the gratification of our selfish wants rule, we see that pain and brokenness abound, rather than more fulfilling relationships. The "evil" of lust is just that: evil. It is contrary to the truth and goodness of the other person. As St. Francis de Sales once said, "take care to admit no evil love because you will soon become evil yourself." Authentic love demands investment *in the person*, and therefore is never fleeting, whether the relationship is romantic or not.

---

85   Cfr. Cyber Parent, *Boundaries in Romantic Relationships*, November 2016, https://cyberparent.com/relationships/boundaries-in-romantic-relationships.

A second danger in this early stage of human love is the idealization of the other. In fact, St. John Paul II says our sentiments, as a rule, "can exaggerate the value of the person out of all proportion to his or her real value....and [values] are bestowed upon the object of love which he or she does not necessarily possess in reality. These are ideal values, not real ones."[86] If love as desire stagnates in idealizing the other or never progresses beyond "I want you because you are a good *for* me," then it is false love. It is not enough to say, "You are a good for me." This is clearly just self-centered. For love to be true, it needs to be expressed as "I long for *your* good, not just my own." This is why our emotional states need the critical test of reason to confirm *as reality* what we feel.

Emotional chastity is the acid test for a mature authentic love. Pausing and reflecting can speak truth into emotionally blind situations. One practical way to be sure that the head and heart are connecting at this desire-love stage is to review 1 Corinthians 13:4-7. Many who have been to Christian weddings have heard this reading, which speaks of the key expressions of true Christian love.[87]

> "*Love is patient; love is kind; love is not envious or boastful or arrogant or rude. It does not insist on its own way; it is not irritable or resentful; it does not rejoice in wrongdoing but rejoices in the truth. It bears all things, believes all things, hopes all things, endures all things.*"

Why is this reading so popular? Without any question it is because the bride and the groom desire to love each other this way and desire to be loved this way by the other. It speaks to our true longings and also gives us a standard for which to strive. Based on this reading, the following questions below may help

---

86 Wojtyla, *Love and Responsibility*, 112.
87 1 Corinthians 13 is understood by many scholars to be an ancient Christian hymn to Christ. It is an "hymn" of praise to him who models the way of authentic self-gift love for us.

ensure that your attraction and desire do not idealize the person you love, and that you are anchored in the whole truth of who they are. If you answer yes to the questions, then your love is on solid realistic footing. If you answered "no" to any of the questions, then maybe you should make it a point to discuss those issues with the person in question.

- Are you patient with each other?
- Are you kind to each other?
- Are you ever envious of each other?
- Do you never boast to or about each other?
- Is your relationship characterized by humility?
- Are you ever rude to each other?
- Are you not self-seeking?
- Are you not easily angered with each other?
- Do you protect each other?
- Do you keep no record of wrongs?
- Are you truthful with each other?
- Do you trust each other?

Emotional chastity promotes self-awareness and the ability to discern well our emotional world so we can avoid the pitfalls of using another person. We are persons and not "playthings." Each has uniqueness that merits respect and deference. Maturing human love does begin with that first "spark" brought on by particular qualities of the other, but moves beyond attraction and desire. Emotional chastity allows the natural course of emotional connection to take place, but monitors that connection with the precision of reason, moving from the tendency to focus on a specific quality to the value of the whole person. Do I want the true good for this person?

This is the third stage of love—and it is called *love as good will*. Goodwill is the next stage and says, "Hmm, I want *your* good."

Small Group Questions:
1. Why can this stage of desire-love, going from "I like" to "I want," be so dangerous?
2. Do our strong desires for another person disqualify or overwhelm our capacity to reason through them?
3. How does emotional chastity differ from the repression of desires?

Going Deeper: What is it about 1 Corinthians 13 that resonates with every person? Read these verses and discuss.

Third Stage: Love as Goodwill

The third stage of human love is goodwill-love. Love as goodwill is free of self-interest. It is not a "I long for you as a good," but rather "I long for *your* good."[88] There is no personal consideration or ulterior motives. Consider, for example, the couple facing the dilemma of being in a "long distance relationship," both with good jobs and yet not quite ready to marry. Who will be the sacrificial lamb and give up a job and perhaps family and friends to move to where the other is located? If goodwill-love is present, then such a situation finds a peaceful resolution with no regret or resentment.

"Reciprocity" is part of goodwill-love and means mutual dependence, forming a "we." It expresses a unique communion, not two loves of two separate independent people, but one united love. St. John Paul II says goodwill-love helps both parties mature to their fullest human potentials.[89] Goodwill-love desires reciprocity and is essential to the question of trust. In

---
88 Wojtyla, *Love and Responsibility*, 83.
89 Cfr., Wojtyla, *Love and Responsibility*, 82-84.

other words, we begin to trust the other when we see the same level of commitment.

The popular romance movie "A Walk to Remember" shows the transforming power of goodwill-love. The protagonist is a "bad boy" in the local high school who falls in love with the pastor's daughter. He learns what authentic love is through a discussion of 1 Corinthians 13. The couple live a pure relationship and strive to form that faithful "we," based on seeking the good of the other.

The opposite of goodwill-love, on the other hand, is often called "unrequited love."[90] It is when one party does all the giving and goodwill-love breaks down. Reciprocity is weakened and trust becomes artificial. For example, in my many hours of talking to unmarried couples, some of whom are living together or have lived with another person, I have witnessed this type of unrequited love. This is perhaps why cohabitation is often called a commitment to a non-commitment. One party, sadly very often the woman, enters into a new stage of the relationship with different expectations than the other party. As one friend told me, the woman, seeking stability and security in her life, perhaps thinks, "If I live with him, this is the right next step to marriage." Meanwhile, the man is thinking, "Sure I care about her and maybe we can make this work, but I am good the way we are right now." Other than trying to be aware of and caring for the other's needs at a basic level, nothing really changes for him.

As one young woman put it, "It was like we were both caring for the same person—him. I felt left out of it."[91] One author explains well this unrequited love reality of cohabitation:

---
90 Wojtyla, *Love and Responsibility*, 85.
91 Evert, *Pure Womanhood*, 17.

> *Sexual intimacy outside of marriage can create an impression of a closeness that does not really exist between people. In their bodies they say, "I'm totally yours." But in reality, their hearts merely say, "I'm yours.... until someone better comes around." In such a relationship, the other person is not truly committed to you as a person. They are more committed to the sensual pleasure and emotion they derive from you. And they could just as easily get their sexual and emotional needs met from someone else down the road. The lack of committed love breeds fear and insecurity."*[92]

A cohabitation relationship oftentimes happens through a "sliding process" without any deliberation. Let's just be brutally honest: One person lives the commitment in a way that is "all in," almost as if they were in a marital state, while the other continues to live as if they were just "roommates." Once the rationalizing of the other's behavior and the fear of "drawing the line" sets in (because that would be the real test of love), mutual benefit breaks down and mistrust enters. As one girl said, "If you have to give a guy something sexual to keep him, you are going to lose him anyway, because he doesn't really love you."[93] Despite the trend, the current studies are wildly clear: Cohabitation does not accomplish the goal of a long term commitment of love. Rather, there are increased risk of divorce, lower quality of marriage, poorer marital communication, and higher levels of domestic violence.[94]

Unanswered questions will continue to abound: How much can I really hope to experience the total love I long for in this

---
[92] Sri, *Unveiled Love*, 252-253.
[93] Evert, *Pure Womanhood*, 19.
[94] Aaron Ben-Zeev, "Does Cohabitation Lead to More Divorces?" *Psychology Today*, March 2013, https://www.psychologytoday.com/us/blog/in-the-name-love/201303/does-cohabitation-lead-more-divorces.

concrete situation? Can I entrust myself to this person, as I truly am, and yet not receive the same in return? How can this relationship bring me the future happiness that I desire?

If the love is based on self-interest, it is condemned to stagnation, then to gradual extinction. True love, by its very nature, is not unilateral. It is bilateral, something that is shared. If reciprocity is present, goodwill-love can come to full maturity.

Small Group Questions:
1. What is goodwill-love? What does it desire for "the other"?
2. Can you have goodwill-love when you are cohabitating and not married?

Going Deeper: Discuss the practical reasons for why cohabitation seems to make sense. Why then do sociological studies show a higher divorce rate for couples who live together before being married? What is the disconnect?

Fourth Stage: Love as Unconditional

A fully mature love is like a synthesis of the first three stages of love. It harmonizes attraction, desire, and goodwill and culminates in this last stage called unconditional love or, as we have been calling it, love as self-gift. This love does more than any other to perfect the persons who experience it and brings the subject and object of that love the greatest fulfillment.[95] Love as self-gift is our ideal and it is a coming together, a unification of persons—truly going from "I" to "we." It is the sharing of one's own person with another. The essence of gift love is

---
95 Wojtyla, *Love and Responsibility*, 84.

surrender— the surrendering of one's "I." None of the other stages of human love can take a human being on his quest for the good of the other as does love as self-gift. It is in this last stage that one says: "I want your good *no matter what* it costs."

How contrary is this view to what we currently see happening in so many relationships! The momentary sentimental love of Katy Perry's song "Teenage Dream" comes nowhere close to the surrender of self-gift love:

> Let's go all the way tonight
> No regrets, just love
> We can dance until we die
> You and I, we will be young forever
> You make me feel like I'm living a, teenage, dream
> The way you turn me on
> I, can't, sleep
> Let's runaway
> And don't ever look back
> Don't ever look back

With unconditional love, short-term satisfaction is not the goal. Personal wants and needs become secondary and one is willing to embrace sacrifices, inconveniences, or troubles necessary for the good of the other. There can be no true love without some suffering, because authentic love always implies renouncement of self, a letting go of "me," and an acceptance of the other as he or she is. It implies a coming out of self for the other. This final stage of love is echoed in the powerful words of St. John Paul II: The person who does not decide to love forever will find it very hard really to love even for one day.[96] Love as self-gift expresses this desire to love forever and as not just one more superficial event in the life of a person.

---
96   Ibid., 171.

Self-gift love is most perfectly expressed through the public promises one makes when committing to the state of marriage or consecrated life. The fullness of human love is not compatible with "trial" marriages or commitments. Rather, it demands a surrender, a total and definitive gift of a person to another. But one might ask, is it even possible to surrender oneself totally to another? In the physical order, the very nature of the person is incompatible with such a surrender—for example, to become someone else's property. Nobody can be transferred to another as a possession. However, what is impossible in the merely physical order is possible in the order of love, indicating the special dynamism of the human person.

Here, we see in all its radiance the capacity of the human person for perfection, proceeding step by step with love—our highest and most noble aspiration. For example, through making a free choice to publicly commit to marriage, rather than being somehow limited or weakened by the act, the person is actually enriched and made more perfect. How? The committed state challenges you to invest and stay the course in a relationship that offers a path toward ever greater perfection. "It is precisely in suffering this surrender, caused by the losing of self for the sake of the other, for the loved one, that I become great and my life finds love, and in love finds its meaning."[97] Hence when we give of ourselves totally to another, rather than lose something, we end up gaining everything. We "recover" our true selves.

Is there any wonder why within the marital state the one physical act that communicates this total surrender of self is called "making love"? In light of this, the use of artificial contraception makes no sense and contradicts the physical act. Why do we want to block the spirit of self-gift that such an

---

97   Pope Benedict, Meeting of the Holy Father Benedict XVI with the Clergy of the Dioceses of Belluno-Feltre, July 2007, https://www.catholic.org/featured/headline.php?ID=4710.

act expresses? In the end, the contraceptive sex act says "I cannot entrust my total self to you," whether we desire to say this or not.

As with contraception, distrust is also the problem with cohabitation. It seems intuitive and even prudent that two people should live together before making the very serious and lifelong commitment of marriage. Living together to discover if, in fact, they are "really" compatible, makes sense, right? However, the statistics say the opposite. Those who live together before marriage divorce at a higher rate once married. Why? One could argue that the reason is that cohabitation does not begin with the bedrock of trust as marriage does; rather, it begins with a certain suspicion that "we may not be right for each other, so let's test this." Two individuals *hope* they might "be right for each other" but suspect it is a real possibility they may not be, for any number of reasons. This is a different mindset from the couple who know there will be challenges, yet their common commitment to a higher ideal of permanency in marriage, aided by God's grace and the community, assures them they *can* be faithful. The institution of marriage expresses just this: you vow publicly before each other and the community, *trusting* that with the help of God and your community, both persons will persevere "till death do us part." When a couple commits to this ideal publicly before those who are most vested in helping them, statistics support that this is of huge benefit to the couple and to the entire human community.

Cohabitation also does not reflect the *totality* of the love that self-gift communicates. "Total" means the *whole* human picture. Excluding the support of your community, family, and God is foolishness. Nevertheless, those who live together say just that: "We are going to try to make this work," as if two very imperfect people have any chance to make it work on their own. Cohabitation is a "horizontal" commitment with little "vertical" dependence on the grace of God and family to help a couple push through the normal valleys of marital relations.

In other words, when a couple has a shared orientation toward a common ideal of marriage, they begin their life together with a total YES to this ideal. Not living together before marriage is already a shared sacrifice that they both make, a shared act of love of waiting for something so good, until God and the community blesses it. This dynamic of generous and sacrificial self-gift is the best preparation for marriage. Foregoing this for what is more expedient or practical is missing a chance to build their relationship on rock.

This lifelong commitment to self-gift love is beautiful to experience and beautiful to see in others. When we catch sight of it, there is a specific radiance. It speaks to our hearts. It reminds me of a Mass I celebrated once for a couple that had been married for fifty years. They were like innocent children interacting with each other—innocent and pure. This is what unconditional love does: It stops us in our tracks. We are wowed by it.

Small Group Questions:

1. How does unconditional love perfect the person who loves? How does it perfect the other?
2. Why does waiting to live together before marriage strengthen a couple's relationship?
3. Discuss why contraception and cohabitation are fundamentally based on distrust.

Going Deeper: Name a married couple in your life who have been a great example of faithful, unconditional love.

Conclusion of Stages of Love

The four stages of love are necessary steps to reach the fullness of human love and they mature over time, with a lot of mistakes in between. Emotional chastity is not about "stamping out" the good desire in me. It is *not* one long *no*. It is, on the contrary, a yes![98] It is a yes to the value of the person in all that he or she is: body, smile, personality, intelligence, imperfections, everything! Everything in us gets directed to the value of the person rather than suppressed. In 2014 the song *All of Me* by John Legend topped the charts in eight countries and seems to touch on that inviolable goodness of the *complete other* that we long to love as a gift.

> "'Cause all of me
> Loves all of you
> Love your curves and all your edges
> All your perfect imperfections
> Give your all to me
> I'll give my all to you
> You're my end and my beginning
> Even when I lose I'm winning
> 'Cause I give you all, all of me
> And you give me all, all of you"

We can meaningfully direct all our vital energies to the good of the other. Emotional chastity is creative as well—helping train our natural reactions, redirecting them perhaps from an initial *me-centered-taking* to a gradual *other-centered-giving*, resulting in respect and recognition of the other. There are not just two choices in my attraction and desire for another person—repression or indulgence. No! There *is* a middle ground, and I can know this and freely choose it!

---

[98] Wojtyla, *Love and Responsibility*, 170.

NOTES

CHAPTER FIVE: WHAT LOVE IS NOT

Living emotional chastity calls one to strive for a love that is a gift of self which harmonizes the head and the heart. We need to see the living witness of it in others, so that we know what we are striving for. Hence, we take a moment now to summarize this love that emotional chastity seeks to foster—to paint a true picture of its principle characteristics so that we have a clear understanding of this type of love and can avoid the counterfeits. We come closer to that true picture by explaining what love is NOT.

Self-gift love is *not* merely a human thing. Love is so vital to who we are, to our happiness as finite creatures. Our Creator-God, who is Mystery, perfect Truth, and Goodness, is essentially this: Love. *The human images the Divine.* Our very human existence is meant to reflect the expression of love as God is. This is why the Pope calls the human person a *sign*.[99] How we live our lives as male and female, essentially how we love, can be a living breathing *signpost* to the world, a pathway of love for others that leads to a meaningful and purposeful life.

Self-gift love is *not* conditional. *It is total.* It is "all in." In fact, our male-female body-person experience speaks of this: *being a total gift* to the other. *Gift* is written into the physical make-up of our male-female complementarity. The fitting together of man and woman communicates this language of gift. St. John Paul II called this male-female bodily imprint the *spousal meaning of the body*, which refers to the body's language to express

---

[99] "The Creator has assigned the body to man as a task, the body in its masculinity and femininity... he assigned to him in some way his own humanity as a task, that is, the dignity of the person and also the transparent sign of interpersonal 'communion' in which man realizes himself through the authentic gift of self." St. John Paul II, *Theology of the Body*, 59.

love. Only the human body is capable of making visible in this most intimate human act what is invisible. That is how the persons of the Trinity love one another with Divine totality. The invisible (Divine love) is made visible (human love) through the physical (human body).

Self-gift love is *not* singular. If human love is modeled on Divine love which flows from the Trinity, a family of persons (Father, Son, Holy Spirit), then true human love must be more than just about *me*. It is plural; it is *other*-centered. We are not islands. Human beings live in relationship. It does not just bring more than one person together, but brings people into a profound communion. St. John Paul II called it a communion of persons. Relationships are investments. They require time and energy.

Self-gift love is *not* using the other. Rather, it honors the goodness and mystery of the other. Reverence and devotion for the other person is the proper response between man and woman. Each sex has its own equal, complementary dignity. Living in accordance with the way we are made and respecting it is, ultimately, the source of our happiness and social well-being.

Self-gift love is *not* disembodied. In fact, it simply cannot be. Love is not merely something spiritual but a body-spirit union involving our entire human embodiment. Both the body and the spirit influence the other. We cannot do whatever we want with our body and think it will not affect other areas of our *persona*. If we choose to expose our bodies to harmful experiences, there will be painful consequences affecting "all of me."

Self-gift love is *not* merely a fleeting emotion. Rather, it communicates something eternal. This is why most lovers often think, "This will last forever," because the intensity of the experience says, "I am totally for you, holding nothing back, forever!" The words of Pope Francis capture the essence of this fact:

> *"Lovers do not see their love as merely temporary. Those who marry do not expect their excitement to fade. Those who witness the celebration of a loving union, however fragile, trust that it will stand the test of time."*[100]

Self-gift love is *not* completed by another human being in this life. St. John Paul II refers to this *heart-intuition* of perfect eternal love as that *echo* of the original beginning when the first man and woman were created for God. Even when disordered love (sin) entered the world, this echo, this desire in us for perfect love, remained. The echo of perfect love awakens in each other a thirst, a desire for fullness *out of proportion* with their capacity to quench it for the other. However, the fact remains, both male and female are limited. Only the perfect love of God can truly respond to this echo.

As partners in life (Genesis 2:20), each is meant to help point the other to where they can find this fulfillment that the other has aroused. "This is the paradox of love between man and woman. Two infinities meet two limitations, the two infinite needs to be loved meet two fragile and limited capacities to love."[101] Only in the orbit of a greater love, Divine love, do man and woman not consume themselves in a false hope that the hunger will go unsatisfied, but they walk with each other toward that near perfect love.

---

100 Pope Francis, *Amor Laetitia*, 123.
101 Father Carron, as quoted in *Magnificat*, December 30, 2018, 449-450.

In the end, followers of Christ know that there is a perfect lover. Life teaches us that *"by falling in love, one realizes that all one's happiness is bound up with 'somebody'. And it is often only after the comparative failure of that 'somebody' that one learns to know the real 'somebody' who is Christ. The seeming inability of the other person to return the love given—leads one to look further for the perfect lover–the tremendous lover–who is Christ."*[102] This is a mystery that our minds could never have dreamt up unless it was revealed to us. "No one has ever seen God. It is God the only Son, who is close to the Father's heart, who has made him known" (John 1:18). The yearning for more, the restlessness, the desire to be completed by another—these human experiences are but the seeds of the Divine echo in our hearts that God placed there from the very beginning. He created us to be filled, not empty. "I have come to bring you life and life to the full" (John 10:10). St. Augustine sums it up well: "My heart is restless until it rests in you."

To sum up: Dependence on God by we human beings is born solely from the love that he has for us, while the dependence of human beings among ourselves is born from the need we have for one another.

Small Group Questions:
1. Discuss how the Blessed Trinity loves like a family.
2. How is Jesus Christ the answer to the restlessness in the human heart?

Going Deeper: Discuss the words: "Two infinities meet two limitations; the two infinite needs to be loved meet two fragile and limited capacities to love." Can another human being fulfill you?

---

102 Eugene Boylan, *This Tremendous Lover* (Cork, Ireland: Mercier Press, 1964), 316.

NOTES

CHAPTER SIX: WHAT INHIBITS LIVING EMOTIONAL CHASTITY?

If doing whatever you like without any discernment is the way to go, then why are so many unhappy?

It takes much effort in the ambit of human love to choose rightly. There is that constant voice inside us, and all around us, that blares the message "go for it," regardless of consequences. There are many factors that bring about bad decisions in the arena of human love; many of which are deep in the human heart. Consider the story of the teenage girl Mary Jane. She grew up in a typical churchgoing middle-class family from the Midwest. She even participated in the Wednesday night youth group. However, her father was absent from her life for the most part. He was never really able to connect with her. The family moved to another city, couldn't find a church community they liked, changed schools a few times, and by her senior year, with the encouragement of her friends, falls in love and finds herself pregnant with the first boy who showed her some love and attention.

Within this story, one can find the obstacles to living emotional chastity today: a) our human frailty, b) the de-humanizing secular culture around us, and c) other forces hostile to the good of the person.

Human Frailty

Human frailty is the first obstacle to living emotional chastity. As we have seen, love is probably the most important human experience. Few would disagree with the statement that all human beings long for love. We need love in our lives—to give and receive love. Yet when we try to love another person, it is not always trouble-free. It seems to cost us effort—at times a lot of effort. In fact, the human person is not always so lovable. Few things appear to be "true" today for everyone. Human frailty is true for all, however, for every human person is weak and imperfect.

Something is not right with us. For clarity sake, let's call this "something" a self-centered spirit. More often than not, our interior motives can be self-seeking, even perverse. We are all looking out for number one! Consequently, our external actions are very imperfect and unsatisfactory, especially in regard to loving another person.

This is not new to humanity—2,500 years ago, the Greek philosopher Plato described human nature like a spirited horse. It must be controlled at every step. It likes to run free and wild. Hence, we need not be surprised at our changing feelings and moods. Yet all the while, we know these inner attitudes are often not our "better" self. Too frequently, we fail to put up a fight against our "me-centered" feelings and blind desires. At other times, we try to fight them alone. Or what is worse, we are so often unaware of these selfish tendencies because our self-awareness is so poor.

Those who profess a faith in God know the diagnosis. For at least three millennia, the Judaic, followed by the Christian tradition, referred to this human experience as *iniquity* or the consequences of sin. The rupture that took place between our first parents and their Creator, God, also fractured the harmony and wholeness within the human person, causing inner rebellion. It is like the hard drive in us was damaged. The light of reason is darkened, our will and its capacity to choose the good is weakened, and the world of our emotions has gone silly. Rather than whole human beings, we are broken and fragmented.

Chapter Six: What Inhibits Living Emotional Chastity?

Sin is a word that has been denied, rebuked, chided, censured, admonished, and forgotten. The word "sin"[103] can be traced back to the Hebrew word *hattah*, which actually originates in archery and literally refers to hitting the target but missing the "gold" at the center of a target. To sin literally means *to miss the mark*. What mark would that be? Perhaps the mark of inner peace. Sin takes away our inner peace, and peace is the consequence when everything is in its right place, when harmony reigns. This is not a temporary feeling of peace which seems to rationalize an uneasy conscience. No, it is an enduring peace, a peace that persists in good times and in bad. "If you have that peace, you no longer feel like a collection of scattered pieces. You have become *whole*."[104]

This notion of sin had to be revealed to us by God because sin is not always recognizable and we are tempted to explain it as merely a flaw, psychological weakness, or mistake. It sounds much like the alcoholic who says, "I don't have an issue" and yet everything and everyone around him says otherwise. No other human tradition in history has such a complete explanation on sin expressed in human frailty than the Judeo-Christian one. It says that, "Only in the knowledge of God's plan for man can we grasp that sin is an abuse of the freedom that God gives to created persons so that they are capable of loving him and loving one another."[105]

Sin is possible only because God is love, and since love must be free, it includes the possibility of rebellion, of refusal, of rejection.

---

103 *CCC* 1849 defines sin as "an offense against reason, truth, and right conscience; it is failure in genuine love for God and neighbor caused by a perverse attachment to certain goods. It wounds the nature of man and injures human solidarity."
104 Wilfred Stinnisen, *Holy Spirit, Fire of Divine Love* (San Francisco: Ignatius Press, 2017), 87.
105 See *CCC* 387. The human heart battles with what is called "concupiscence": the disordered desire for pleasure, turning the love of the body into "bodily love." It is not sin but an inclination toward it.

God created us to freely love him and others. Remember the first commandment? Because we are free, we also are free to reject him. When we misuse our freedom and love selfishly, or use the other person, then an inner civil war ensues, and relationships suffer.

This is where St. John Paul II emphatically responds that it is precisely within the sacred "space" of our hearts that we must rediscover what is lost–what has gone missing–and want to regain it.[106] He describes it as *our lost fullness of humanity*. We have lost our fullness. In fact, it is expressed in us more as a sort of emptiness, an ache within us that we desperately want to fill. We ache because we are not full. Perhaps this is why we are not content with just one experience of *anything*. If *just one* of these thrills that we seek did actually fill us, we would stop with it, rest with it, be content with it. Our endless seeking would end. But it never does!

Sin does not fill us; it empties us because it damages our ability to relate to others. It harms the unity between people. It is more of a closing-off than an opening-up. Conversely, making oneself a gift to the other *does* fill us. To sincerely give and receive love with no regard to self—this is our greatest satisfaction! To quote the words so dear to the heart of St. John Paul II, "The human person cannot fully find himself except through a sincere gift of self."[107]

To love as a total gift of self is what makes us *most* human, and so we need to learn how to love like this. In this light, emotional chastity demands effort and precisely a lot of practice because it forges in us this responsible love. Our happiness depends on it.

---

106 Cfr. St. John Paul II, *Theology of the Body*, 43, 7.
107 *Gaudium et Spes*, 24.

Small Group Questions:
1. What do we mean when we say "something is not right with us"?
2. What is sin? Why do you think the concept of sin is so often rejected today?

Going Deeper: Name some examples in your life that prove these words true: "Sin does not fill us; it empties us."

Dehumanizing Secular Culture

THE MATERIALIZING OF LOVE

The second inhibiting factor to living emotional chastity is our current secular culture.

Secular means worldly or irreligious. It is a culture imploding on itself because the sense of God and the dignity of his creation, particularly the human person, is of no importance. We may not always be aware of it because we are so immersed in it. The film *No Strings Attached* is a perfect example of the secular "disposable" culture and its influence on human love. Two friends try to just "hook up" casually, but in the end it's too hard not to actually "feel" for the other, so they end up together. The film depicts well how the hookup culture is essentially a lie. When you engage in physical intimacy, it affects the person on multiple levels, body and soul. The objectification of another person, as just one more *thing* to use and then be discarded, carries with it terrible consequences. The sociological data on this damaging phenomenon is crazy: depression, suicide, violence, substance abuse, and the list goes on.[108] We could call this the materializing of love.

---
108 Laird, B. (May 28, 2013). Uncoupling the hookup culture. Retrieved April 2, 2017, from http://articles.latimes.com/2013/may/28/opinion/la-oe-laird-hookup-culture-20130528.

The greatest impact of this materializing of love is on human beings themselves. Persons are disposable. "We treat affective relationships the way we treat material objects and the environment: everything is disposable; everyone uses and throws away, takes and breaks, exploits and squeezes to the last drop. Then, goodbye. Narcissism makes people incapable of looking beyond themselves, beyond their own desires and needs."[109]

Each sex can manifest narcissistic behavior in different ways. "Men are likely to emphasize intellect, power, aggression, money, or social status. Women are likely to emphasize body, looks, charm, sexuality, feminine "traits", homemaking, children, and childrearing."[110] For a man this can translate into: go and dominate, control, conquer, take what others will give you in business or in love. For women, it looks like: do anything to feel loved, secure, noticed, and desired, and do whatever is necessary to keep this feeling of love. Perceived self-worth is often be based on material and social factors.

Lifelong fidelity to one person is not possible or desired. "Too many headaches to be with the same person all your life." "We can always start all over again" when love becomes not fun. "It is the culture of the ephemeral…the speed with which people move from one affective relationship to another. They believe, along the lines of social networks, that love can be connected or disconnected at the whim of the consumer, and the relationship quickly 'blocked'."[111] Truly this is the materializing of love.

---

[109] Pope Francis, *Amoris Laetitia*, 39.
[110] Vaknin, S. (November 16, 2008). Gender and the Narcissist - Female Narcissist, Healthy Place. Retrieved May 4, 2020, from https://www.healthyplace.com/personality-disorders/malignant-self-love/gender-and-the-narcissist.
[111] Ibid.

Small Group Questions:
1. What is the meaning of the phrase "secular culture"?
2. What is "the materializing of love"? Name some examples in your life.

Going Deeper: Discuss this statement: "Narcissism makes people incapable of looking beyond themselves, beyond their own desires and needs." Do you believe this to be true? Have you ever experienced this type of behavior?

THE CYCLE OF USING

These two factors together, human frailty and its tendency to be self-serving, along with the "materializing power" of the secular culture, create what could be called *the cycle of using* within human relationships.[112] The cycle is a strong tendency to seek a certain emotional experience, but once it is reached and loses its luster, the cycle starts again. This can happen virtually—in one's mind—or in real relationships. Within relationships of love, two people end up mutually using the other emotionally, physically, or very often both. The cycle looks different in men and women. Though for one person it may be more physical and for the other more emotional, both are seeking some form of gratification at the expense of the other.

At the core of the cycle of using is the human heart that battles with disordered desires for pleasure, turning the love of the body into "bodily love." The fascinating thing is that just as both the male and female body reflect the total gift of self in love, so too the disordered love of using another is expressed in the makeup of the human body. For example, the male sex organs are *external* to his body, whereas for a woman, they are *internal*. The appearance of disordered love, like lust, is quite often

---
[112] Cfr. Sara Swafford, *Emotional Virtue* (Scottdale, AZ: Totus Tuus Press, 2014), 36.

detected because it is *externalized* in male behavior: the gawking at a woman's body, the vulgar verbalization of the same, and the acting out of what is seen in movies or pornography. Such expressions are all very common in male behavior, but generally not in female behavior. Women, on the contrary, most often fight their battles, not in the external but the *internal*: in their thoughts and imagination, and in the illusion of love.

Just as the obvious external expression of objectifying the other as a mere object of use is readily recognizable as disordered, why wouldn't the internal reality be just as dangerous? Since this internal phenomenon appears to be less obvious to people, consider some examples that many women have shared with me in my ministry as a priest:

- Being all-consumed with her personal Pinterest collection of pictures, videos, and other things used to escape the reality of her current state in life.
- Obsessing over her personal social media posts, wanting to intrigue other followers.
- Daydreaming about guys she may not even know and allowing emotions to attach to someone or a situation that is outside of one's reality.
- Idolizing relationships in movies, leading to disappointment when a guy does not live up to those unrealistic expectations; binging on chick flicks.
- Hesitating to develop healthy relationships with the opposite sex to avoid obsessive and delusional thinking about them.
- Desiring to be seen or be noticed by men, which manifests itself in dressing a certain way.
- Sleeping with a guy because she hopes that he will stay interested in her.

Chapter Six: What Inhibits Living Emotional Chastity?

- Going to strip clubs or watching porn with a man because she feels that is what she has to do to be desired.
- Within marriage: fantasizing about the ideal man who totally fulfills his wife, perfectly meeting all her needs as provider, protector, lover, and dad.

Both men and women fall into seeking gratification from the other. This behavior has become so normalized that few really see it as hurting themselves or others. This happens not only in romance, but in all relationships. How many parents have commented to me about their deep sadness at how their children only really talk to them when they *want* something?

Many chastity speakers today mention manifestations of this problem. One quick way to snap yourself out of this cycle is to think about a time when you felt used. Chastity speaker Sara Swafford speaks of this and asks:

- Think about a time when you used another person.
- Think about a time when you saw another person being used.
- Think about a time when you saw a person using another person.

These are questions that challenge all of us because, unfortunately, the very air we breathe is filled with it.

As we have seen, we are embodied persons, designed to be a gift, given and received. We express our love through the body in so many ways. Yet, sin subverts that Divine design, and the disorder that comes through lusting after the other is also expressed in some form through the body. Is there any wonder why so much hurt points to the body? How often is the body blamed, rejected, or degraded? We are not meant to despise our bodies, but rather to appreciate them as good and to hold them in honor.

Small Group Questions:
1. What does the cycle of use mean? Have I seen this in my own behavior? Have I ever felt used?
2. Discuss the different expressions of lust in a man or woman.

Going Deeper: Discuss the above points mentioned by Sara Swafford that help to snap oneself out of a cycle of using.

THE LIE OF ABSOLUTE FREEDOM

Where there is false freedom, there is false love. Disordered expressions of human love continue primarily because of misunderstandings about human freedom. Freedom is an absolute value today. Leaving your options *open* is an imperative. This false notion of freedom is so unqualified, and personal independence is so absolute, that any guidelines which are in the least bit normative are negative and obstruct our freedom to choose. Yet every choice brings with it some type of sacrifice—something you *did not* choose and have to give up. You cannot get around it. Hence why this current spirit of absolute freedom is based on a lie. It does not really exist.

Expression of this misplaced notion of freedom can also be seen in the mentality that exists toward forms of long-term commitment. Such relationships today are considered a real hindrance, damaging to one's freedom, even at the cost of a truly fulfilling relationship. For example, when one commits to another person in marriage, certain freedoms are sacrificed (yet other goods are acquired). The loss of freedom, nonetheless, seems to be the only thing one refers to nowadays when it comes to committing to marriage. It is even worse when it comes to having children! However, we *do* win in marriage. It *does* bring important benefits to each party. Marriage simply makes the other a better person. It is the perfecting of one's love for the other, from selfish to more selfless. Does this not have any value?

The secular notion of this unqualified freedom finds its most extreme expression in seeing the human person as gender-fluid. The new gender theory essentially sees the human body as merely a *shell* encompassing our "real self." This dangerous trend says we can choose to follow a deep feeling of attraction to be male or female regardless of our original sex, even though our very biology says we are male or female. "Such theories deny the difference and reciprocity in nature of man and woman and envisage a society without sexual difference, thereby eliminating the anthropological basis of the family."[113]

The human body, however, is more than a covering; it is the physical manifestation of our personhood. As one psychologist aptly described this point:

> *"Our bodies are integral manifestation of who we are as human beings. Our bodies are not something we have, but something we are. Our deepest human identity is that of an embodied person: our bodies are not unspecified but have certain characteristics that constitute who we are, for example, being male or female. The popular sense is that the self is contained within the body, but the truth is that we are our bodies. If our human dignity flows from being made in the image of God and therefore we are good, then our bodies are*

---

[113] Pope Francis, *Amoris Laetitia*, 54.

therefore good. To ignore or avoid them is to avoid something of God".[114]

One example of how our human embodiment connects us to our identity besides the most obvious—a woman having a baby—is breastfeeding. Since the identity of a woman *includes all of her*, body and soul, one could argue that her external, physiological ability to breastfeed reveals the inner wiring of her feminine gift to nurture, empathize, and intuit the thoughts and emotions of others. This behavior is part and parcel of the gift of her feminine genius, which is centered on relationship and connectivity. This simply is not the case with the male sex.

Our freedom as male or female is to be creative and thrive within the natural bounds of our body-person reality. Yet "when freedom to be creative becomes the freedom to create oneself, then necessarily the Maker himself is denied and ultimately man too is stripped of his dignity as a creature of God."[115] Emotional chastity seeks to foster human creativity within the natural identity of male and female while maintaining one's dignity as a creature of God.

Our development as persons depends strictly on the way we use our freedom, and we are all responsible for our own development as persons. We need to own the process. Our misuse of our freedom has consequences—sometimes tragic ones. We like our freedom, yet we do not always seem to grasp the seriousness of the responsibility that comes with it. The "built-in reluctance to accept responsibility is so much part of fallible human nature. It is not surprising to find it at work in regards to

---

114 Bottaro, *Catholic Mindfulness*, 49-50.
115 Pope Benedict XVI, *Christmas Greetings to the Roman Curia*, December 2012, http://www.vatican.va/content/benedict-xvi/en/speeches/2012/december/documents/hf_ben-xvi_spe_20121221_auguri-curia.html.

our most fundamental task in life: determining what sort of persons we shall be."[116] We are all tempted to deflect our responsibility elsewhere and blame our failures on factors over which we have no control, like our heredity and environment. No doubt there are life issues that might impact us. They can limit our freedom, but not completely. Instead of lamenting over our situation, the challenge is to ask ourselves about those factors that are actually within our control. What are we doing with the freedom that we *do* have?

Small Group Questions:
1. Discuss the false notion of absolute freedom today.
2. Why do some people think a long-term relationship like marriage will inhibit their freedom?
3. Name some examples where the following words play out in your life: "We like our freedom, yet we do not like the responsibilities that come with it."

Going Deeper: How do we speak to someone who sees no problem with gender fluidity? What are the most convincing arguments against it?

The Reality of Evil

The third inhibiting factor to emotional chastity is evil: the wicked forces in the world that are against the good of the human person and ultimately God the Creator. Our present age is an age where "seeing is believing." Anything invisible is discounted as "unreal." Yet evil exists. The devil has acquired a certain domination over man, even though man remains free.[117]

---
116 Griesez and Shaw, *Beyond the New Morality*, 159.
117 *CCC* 407.

Even before being elected Pope John Paul II, Karol Wojtyla did not mix his words about evil and its threat to society:

> "We are now standing in the face of the greatest historical confrontation humanity has gone through. I do not think that wide circles of the American society or wide circles of the Christian community realize this fully. We are now facing the final confrontation between the Church and the anti-Church, of the Gospel and the anti-Gospel. This confrontation lies within the plans of Divine providence. It is a trial which the whole Church... must take up."[118]

Everything that is foundational to healthy human experience, which is good and necessary for an ordered and just society, is now under direct and aggressive scrutiny:

- What it means to be male or female?
- Understanding the human body and sexuality.
- The nature of marriage between one man and one woman.
- The need to continue the human species.

Evil is an active force that perverts the good, and it perverts others. It will always be the perversion of the good, twisting what is good into something it was never meant to be.

Marriage and family life are at the center of this great struggle between good and evil because this is where we learn to love. St. John Paul II expressed it well: "The family is placed at the center of the great struggle between good and evil, between

---

[118] Cardinal Karol Wojtyla, speech to the American Bishops, 1976, reprinted November 9, 1978, issue of *The Wall Street Journal*.

life and death, between love and all that is opposed to love."[119] In other words, where there are men and women, who both image God, the source of all love, there will always be a battle for the good of love.

Small Group Questions:
1. What is evil? Have you ever seen concrete instances of real evil in your life?
2. What does it mean to say that evil twists the good into something that it was never meant to be?

---

[119] St. John Paul II, *Letter to Families*, 23.

NOTES

CHAPTER SEVEN: REDEMPTION

How is healthy human love meant to flourish in today's culture?

Hope is at the center of Christianity. As Christians, we have always believed that there is nothing to prevent our human nature from being raised up to something greater, even after sin. The victory over sin of Jesus Christ, the new Adam, has given us great blessings. Christ has redeemed us and granted to us the power of grace to change our hearts. The law of his Gospel "promises the reform of the heart, the root of human acts" (*CCC* 1984).

The word "redemption" also means to *restore*. Christ restores the original unity to man and to woman that was lost by sin. This restoration allows our human family and our relationships with one another to be seen as gifts rather than as threats. They enrich us and make our human experience better. This was indeed the prevailing spirit of the first Christians: "God has so constructed the body [the Church] that there be no dissension in the body, but that all the members may be concerned for one another. If one member suffers, all the members suffer with it; if one member is honored, all the members share its joy" (1 Corinthians 12:24b, 25-26). Through Christ, the human person, as it were, is given his humanity anew.

Being *discipled* in Christ is a calling and an invitation to conform your life to Christ's own life. It is the imitation of Christ. Following the living Christ is not static; it is a dynamic, life-transforming adventure. The first Christians saw Jesus Christ as a vibrant living person. For example, consider the calling of Matthew, the tax collector (Matthew 9:9). Christ enters into his personal world, right there at the tax collector's office, and invites Matthew to follow him. His response to the call was both immediate and entire. It was a free response that said, "Lord, I say yes to walking with you!"

This is why trying to live emotional chastity is even worth thinking about—we have the very power of God on our side to help us! Christ himself promised this when he said, "I have come to bring you life, and life to the full" (John 10:10). It is through Baptism that our spirits are first awakened to the full reality of this new life and its possibilities.

Small Group Questions:
1. What does Christ's redemption restore to the human person?
2. Is anyone "discipling" you right now in Christ? Why is this important in our Christian walk?

BAPTISM AND THE POWER OF REDEEMING GRACE

The great English Christian apologist Frank Sheed describes redeemed man through the supernatural life in our souls from Baptism. "This life is a new fact, as real as the natural life we have to start with. The powers that Baptism give us are facts too. It enables us to do things that we could not do without them. They are as real as eyesight and considerably more important."[120] What are these new powers, concretely?

- The power of our intellect, which exists to know the truth, is given a new power to know truth in a new way (the gift of faith).
- The power of our will, which exists to love goodness, is given a new power to love in a new way (the gift of hope and love).

---
120 Frank Sheed, *Theology for Beginners* (London: Sheen and Ward, 1958), 71-73.

If this point is not clear, then one will not understand that *literally* we live as Christians in the proportion that we are associated to the *very* life of Christ in us, like the branch to a vine. As the very sap runs through the vine to its branches, so too the power of grace runs from Christ to the rest of us united to him in Baptism.

The first Christians boldly proclaimed this new truth: "If anyone is in Christ, the *new creation* has come: the old has gone, the *new* is here!" (2 Corinthians 5:17). Beginning with Baptism, it is through the sacraments of the Catholic Church that this new life is lived and strengthened in our lives. The regular reception of the sacraments, especially the Eucharist and Reconciliation, assists with the reordering of our fractured human nature and helps bring cooperation between our head and our heart. The new powers of faith, hope, and love redeem man. They *reorder* and *reintegrate* the human person. Redeeming grace brings "light" to our reason, "strength" to our will, and "order" to our emotions. All of me has been redeemed! And this reordering makes for good choices and, therefore, a happier life.

This process of reordering happens according to Christ's dominion in your life. The more his authority grows in breadth and extension into every corner of your life, the quicker the transformation happens. Is he not Lord? Embracing the Cross at the center of the process, we begin to discover the value of suffering. It can be a very positive reality which helps us to mature, to become more ourselves, and to be closer to the Lord who suffered for us and suffers *now* with us. We also need our family and friends and our communities, who inspire us to live a Christ-centered life day by day. We need witnesses, like the examples of the saints and the martyrs, who have given themselves totally, to give us hope that living a Christ-centered life is possible! We need them if we are to prefer goodness to comfort, even in the little choices we face each day, knowing that this is how we live life to the full. Truly, it is a path of purification and growth in maturity. It is a journey of hope.

Small Group Questions:

1. What are the three new powers we receive in Baptism?
2. How does grace actually "reorder" our reason, will, and emotions?

Going Deeper: Do a group Gospel reflection on the words of Jesus: "I am the vine; you are the branches. Those who abide in me and I in them bear much fruit, because apart from me you can do nothing" (John 15: 5).

NOTES

CHAPTER EIGHT: LIVING EMOTIONAL CHASTITY–THE LAW OF GRADUALNESS[121]

Like other good habits, emotional chastity has *laws of growth* which progress through stages marked by imperfection and very often by human weakness (CCC 2343). Good habits, like the virtue of chastity, grow over time. They need repetition to take root. We *gradually* form the good habit of being chaste. The law of gradualness, nonetheless, is not the *gradualness of the law,* as if being chaste is only binding to us after we are mature enough to follow it. With the age of reason comes the understanding of what right behavior is expected of you. We do not strive to be partially chaste. We are either chaste or unchaste. I am not chaste one-third, then one-half, then two-thirds of the time, and so on. While we are conquering a bad habit (vice), with a good habit (virtue), more and more of one's choices are led by reason and faith, and less by instinct and emotion. The habit of emotional chastity is gradually formed by practice. Through the law of gradualness, emotional chastity is nurtured, and self-gift love will mature. It takes time and lots of effort to go from a selfish love to an unselfish love. A positive and dedicated decision to live emotional chastity will eventually bring the sweet joys of peace and freedom.

There are five key components to begin the gradual process of forming this habit of emotional chastity:
1. Develop the capacity for personal reflection: connecting the head and heart.
2. Expose yourself to the sources of sacramental transforming grace.

---

[121] St. John Paul II, *Familiaris Consortio*, (Boston: Daughters of St. Paul, December 1981), 34.

3. Cultivate life-giving relationships.
4. Cultivate life-giving behavior toward others through service to your neighbor.
5. Develop intentional gratitude.

All five of these components help harmonize the human person—reason, will, emotions—through the development of good habits. Good habits make for good choices and choosing the good of the other makes for human flourishing.

Small Group Questions:
1. What is the law of gradualness when it comes to forming good habits?
2. Talk about some of the pitfalls or mistakes that may come along the way of striving to live emotional chastity?

Personal Reflection

Emotional chastity matures through self-discovery, and this cannot happen without personal reflection. When we speak of reflection, we are talking about what makes us most human. It is the capacity to go within oneself, to ponder and consider, to hear oneself think. This is what distinguishes us from the rest of the created animal world and what strengthens our purpose in life. Let's call it the adventure of self-discovery. We remember the famous words of the great Greek philosopher Socrates, "The unexamined life is not worth living." If we can understand, know, and accept ourselves first—this includes what our purpose in life is—this helps us know, understand, and accept the others who we are called to love. Living in a world full of distractions makes it hard to do this very well because, as one poet says, *we are distracted from distraction by distraction.*

Chapter Eight: Living Emotional Chastity—The Law of Gradualness

How does more personal reflection help guide the process of harmonizing our reason, will, and emotions? Personal reflection helps us detect the common danger that St. John Paul II describes as emotional coloring. This coloring is when our emotions seem to mimic our reasoning. Feelings can seem so real and so convincing that we take them for truth itself. It is not that our emotions are not true. They *do* begin in a very real personal experience that demands attention, yet they can balloon into something that is beyond reality. On the one hand, emotions can exhilarate us from "I like him" (normal) to "He is a perfect human being in every way" (impossible!). On the other hand, they can reduce us from "She hurt me" (normal) to "She is the biggest witch I have ever met" (unfair). When we engage more in reflection and less in rash impulsiveness, the powers of our reason can *catch up*, so to speak, and generate light on the concrete matter at hand. Reflection allows us to look at all the factors, not just the strong, overwhelming emotions. This is called self-reflection.

The more we are self-aware and understand what is going on with our emotions and our thinking, the more we can shape and lead them. We need to know where our emotions are leading us. When it is the light of reason that guides our behavior, then this is not repression, but something healthy. We could call it *rational restraint* versus neurotic repression. This is the difference between a healthy and an unhealthy emotional life. In fact, this is emotional chastity in action: the honoring and elevating of our emotions to the light of reason so that we can see and respond freely to what is best for self and best for the other. Truly, this is connecting the head and heart to strive to love in a healthier way.

Here are some more specific suggestions that can further develop the capacity to reflect and help the connection of the head and the heart:

Silence: Reflection is impossible without it. Our very spirits thirst for silence and when we actually get some, wow, what peace we feel in our very souls! The fact that most people in the first world spend up to ten hours a day looking at some form of a screen is very telling. This a lot of visual and mental noise. Modern civilization does not know how to be quiet. We have to build silence into our daily routine and this change can be transformative. (See Appendix I for helpful tips on living silence.)

Prayer: The healthy integration of your rational world (head) with your affective world (heart) cannot take place without prayer. Dramatic things can happen with just a little bit of solitude with Christ. For anyone seeking that internal harmony which we desire, we must learn how to talk and listen to Christ. Communicating with Christ in prayer opens up tremendous self-awareness, because it is Christ who reveals us to ourselves. "Only in this friendship with Christ are the doors of life opened wide. Only in this friendship is the great potential of human existence truly revealed. Only in this friendship do we experience beauty and liberation!"[122]

Thought Management: Emotion can have a powerful sway over our thinking. So much of the level of harmony in the human person comes from how we think, because our thoughts can create havoc or peace in us. So much of what we think about drives our words and actions: fear-filled thinking brings fear-filled actions, and joy-filled thinking brings joy-filled actions. Managing our thinking with more silence and prayer can help give us time to process our thoughts, and this in turn will give us clarity. (See Appendix II for helpful tips on managing our thoughts.)

Study: Coherent sustained thinking and study deepen our capacity to reflect. Yet, they are rare. The digital world so often

---
[122] Pope Benedict XVI, Inauguration of Pope Benedict XVI, Homily, April 24, 2005.

centered on the glitz and glitter that appeals to the senses, brings with it a real resistance to thinking. We are not referring to going over a good idea one heard in one's head, but rather real study and learning: the ordering of data, the evaluation of evidence, and/or following the logical correctness of an argument. Thinking and studying are hard work, and many are not willing to expand the energy or time on them. Through more reflection and study, one develops the spiritual capacity to "see" and process what is going on in the world, rather than simply going from one thing to another. Reflection and study give the interior mental peace for deeper reflection and relationships.

Balance of the Day: Another time-tested way to grow in self-knowledge is called a daily balance. It is an intentional honest review at the end of one's day for ten minutes that asks these questions: "How did my day go today? Why did I do the things that I did today? What did I do well? Where can I improve?" It is so important for every person to be sufficiently present to him or herself in order to hear and follow the voice of conscience (*CCC* 1779). The balance of the day can reveal much about yourself and how God works in your life and in your relationships. How easy it is for us to complain and justify ourselves when we are in conflict with another than to admit our own faults! The daily balance reveals the rights and wrongs and also the patterns and habits that an honest self-assessment can expose. The frequent practice of a balance of the day makes it very difficult to hide our selfishness. This is one of the piercing contrasts between disordered love and genuine love.

Small Group Questions:
1. "The unexamined life is not worth living": Why are these words from the Greek philosopher Socrates relevant to our discussion of emotional chastity?

Going Deeper: Unpack each of the suggestions that develop our capacity to connect the head and the heart: silence, prayer, thought management, study, and balance of the day. Take a moment also to review the appendices for further examples. How do these suggestions help us live intentionally and with purpose, rather than stumbling from day to day with no thought of where life is heading?

Sacramental Life

Emotional chastity is difficult to live without grace: God's life-giving water for the human spirit. The Catholic Church invites her members to go to the sources of sanctifying grace called the sacraments—to encounter Christ in a most powerful and real way. Instituted by Christ, the sacraments are an outward sign of an inward grace. The outward sign is visible and intelligible to our senses, and it gives grace. God desires to reach our very humanity–reason, will, emotions–through what most speaks to us. These visible sacramental signs communicate meaning to our souls and recount our basic human experiences and needs: birth (Baptism), food (Eucharist), forgiveness (Reconciliation), growing in maturity (Confirmation), our chosen state in life (marriage, priesthood, or another form of consecrated life), sickness, and eventually death (Anointing of the Sick). The physical realities used in the sacraments (water, oil, bread, and wine) communicate grace—real Divine power that connects to our sensual human world. Jesus Christ, fully human and fully Divine, knows our human world, opens us up to his Divine world, and wants to meet us right where we are.

My whole self–emotions, senses, reason, will, and body–all of me matters to God, and in turn, should matter to me. When we were baptized, God did not just want us to *understand* his

Chapter Eight: Living Emotional Chastity—The Law of Gradualness

love with just our heads, but also to *feel* it in our bodies when the water splashed to cleanse us from sin. He wants us to *feel* the oil on our heads when anointed in times of illness. In the Sacrament of Reconciliation, through the person of the priest, we *hear* Christ's words of mercy say to us, "I do not condemn you, go your sins are forgiven." And most radically, we *taste and drink* Christ when we literally and mysteriously consume Jesus in the form of bread and wine in the Holy Eucharist.

The fact that we are both body and soul is so important to God that he himself crossed over an infinite distance to become human just like us. The sacramental life is like the difference between looking at a picture and being in the picture. It is living in reality as opposed to watching it.[123] Finally, the sacraments, particularly Holy Eucharist and Reconciliation, are not just a *curative* medicine to help heal the soul from sin but also a *preventative* one. They help us build resistance to sin like taking vitamins helps build up resistance to disease. Emotional chastity is more easily achieved when we invigorate ourselves frequently with the strength of the spirit that God's medicinal grace can give through the sacraments.

The more we are connected to the life-giving grace of the sacraments, the more good habits will develop and grow strong. The very power of God will begin to act within us and illuminate our thoughts, words, and deeds in ever-new ways. "Irresistible grace" does not exist. In other words, we have to freely desire to choose it. A holy man once suggested that to me: "Ask often for the grace of desire." Sanctifying grace begins to heal, elevate, and perfect our very human ways of being, so that we may begin to conform our behavior, to be more like the perfect human being, Christ himself: "The way, the truth, and the life." This is

---

[123] David Morrison, *Beyond Gay* (Huntington, IN: Our Sunday Visitor Publishing, 1999), 190-191. Chapter 12 explains well how very *human* the sacraments are.

what St. Paul called the new man or new woman in Christ. "It is not I, but Christ who dwells within me" (Galatians 2:20).

Finally, there are instances that demand professional attention, such as professional counseling or therapy, as well as God's grace. The human person is frail and broken. In whatever form that may take, mistakes and wounds from our past can have a serious impact on our identity, self-worth, and relationships with others and with God. These wounds can contribute to unhealthy emotional reactions, and impulsive and rash responses, that can hurt us and alienate us from others. Professional help gives us tools to work through and undo the knots in our hearts from bad choices or experiences. After years of pain, becoming aware of the "whys" in our life, and integrating the psychological and spiritual aspects of ourselves, involving family and friends in the process, can be extremely healing to the human person. No one should feel guilty for needing professional help at times.

Small Group Questions:
1. Why did Christ institute the sacraments?
2. How are Holy Communion and Reconciliation like preventive medicine?
3. Talk about how sanctifying grace begins to heal, elevate, and perfect our very human ways.

Going Deeper: Discuss concrete cases where grace is not enough, and professional help should be sought out.

Life-Giving Relationships

Maturing in emotional chastity is necessary for maturing in our relationships. Healthy relationships reform human love from selfish to a more selfless love. The impact of experiencing

Chapter Eight: Living Emotional Chastity—The Law of Gradualness

affirming love authenticates that deep call within me: "I am being loved for my sake, and for no other reason, and I desire to return the love." No man is an island. We need each other. Human interdependence brings human communion and is crucial for our happiness. It is not just functional in nature, but essential. This is why we could identify emotional chastity as a supreme value for learning the art of self-gift love. It affirms our dignity and self-worth. When we are loved in this way, our very being is affirmed: "I am significant, I am good."

Given the current crisis of authentic love, it is also important to name the extreme opposite to life-giving relationships: self-eroticism. It is the attempt to find pleasure and happiness in oneself alone rather than with others. All the facts show that self-eroticism, so often fueled today by various forms of pornography, creates deep personal alienation, self-loathing, and a depletion of one's interpersonal skills. With a cultural epidemic such as pornography comes the common mentality that somehow this isolated act doesn't hurt anyone. This is false. Since love is relational, and relationships involve more than one person, one's personal choices just do not affect just one individual, but the entire vista of who we are and with whom we relate: self, family, and community.

Friendship is the translation for life-giving relationships[124]. The simplest and most straightforward definition of a friend might be someone who cares whether we are around or not. A friend is a person who has a strong liking for and trust in another person. Friends love you and do not use you. Good friends help one regain trust and peace. Developing good friendships takes an *investment* of time and energy—something in our *quick fix* culture that we are not used to doing. It is common knowledge that in our society, we are identifying fewer and fewer people as our "trusted friends,"

---
124 Healthy Lifestyle, *Friendships: Enrich your life and improve your health*, August 24, 2019, https://www.mayoclinic.org/healthy-lifestyle/adult-health/in-depth/friendships/art-20044860.

and the average number is falling quickly[125], while the number of people with no friends is on the increase. Men particularly do not have many friends since, generally speaking, relationship-building skills are weaker in men. Women, on the other hand, have a natural tendency to share. Friendship, either with the same sex or with the opposite sex, is key to good health and the healing of a life that has had to suffer through conflictive relationships.

In a good friendship, friends desire the best for each other, and good friendship so often requires a hard dose of honesty and transparency. True friends should hold each other to higher standards and expect to call each other out when they fall short—not something we like, but we know we need. Our emotional life is an extremely personal and intimate world, especially when it involves others. It falls into the category of *discretionary caution,* and usually only trusted friends have access. However, beware of the tendency to "share everything," because not everyone is going to give you the advice that you should hear or want to hear. The capacity to stop and reflect (rather than react) will help one to ask a most critical question: Who in my life has a right to know about such intimate things? Only time-tested friends.

Small Group Questions:
1. Why are life-giving relationships of supreme value for learning the art of self-gift love?
2. What does it take to be a real friend to another? Name some key characteristics.

Going Deeper: Name examples in your own life of some life-giving relationships. Name some examples of the extreme opposite of life-giving relationships.

---

[125] Jeanna Bryner, Live Science, *Close Friends Less Common Today*, November 4, 2011, https://www.livescience.com/16879-close-friends-decrease-today.html.

Chapter Eight: Living Emotional Chastity—The Law of Gradualness 117

Life-Giving Behavior

Intentional reflection, the active power of Divine grace, and life-giving relationships will result in a deeper contentment and joy. This state of soul will naturally inspire us to share the joy that we have found. It forges convictions in us about serving others and communicates life- giving behavior. This is what happened with the first disciples of Christ. When the apostle Andrew first met Christ, he had an encounter with a special person. This person happened to be the very source of life-giving grace, the God-man Jesus Christ. Through this budding friendship, he immediately went and shared this experience with his brother Peter (John 1:35-42). When something good happens to us, we want to share it.

Life-giving behavior means loving your neighbor through service. It could also be called the power of affirmation. The human person needs to be affirmed by another and made "to feel" valuable. When we seek to serve another, it communicates to the individual, "You are appreciated and good, and I care about you." If to love, and to love well, is the singular most important mission of any human being created by God, then his plan for you is to put your unique gifts to the service of others and to the world! When we choose to act this way towards another person, both parties are affirmed. This is the fruit of authentic love expressed in the joyful service of your neighbor. Pope Francis explains this well: "We become fully human when we become more than human, when we let God bring us beyond ourselves in order to attain the fullest truth of our being. For if we have received the love which restores meaning to our lives, how can we fail to share that love with others?"[126]

---

[126] Pope Francis, *The Joy of the Gospel* (Boston: Pauline Books and Media, 2013), 8-9.

Serving their neighbor helps people discover the fullness of their own mission to love. It helps them overcome the "temptation of selfishness and the subtle danger of seeing their own community as a refuge or a way to flee the problems of the world in an environment of warm friendship."[127] Serving others is a true antidote to selfishness and it matures the fundamental human journey, of going from just "self-discovery," to what we could call "other discovery." Seek to discover your God-given gifts so that you can use them for others. Opportunities to serve abound in your local neighborhoods and communities, not to mention your own church.

Small Group Questions:

1. What is life-giving behavior?
2. How is "serving your neighbor" a recipe for overcoming personal selfishness?

Going Deeper: Have you ever experienced the fruits of being either the giver or the receiver of life-giving behavior? Discuss.

The Power of Intentional Gratitude

We read in the Gospel that only one of the ten lepers healed by Jesus returns to him to give thanks. It seems to be an accurate, but sad indicator about human gratitude: one out of ten on the gratitude scale? We can readily admit that we all take way too much for granted. Gratitude is key to breaking free from a me-centered mindset and progressing to an other-centered mindset. One author describes the positive psychology of gratitude:

---

[127] Archbishop Rylko, *Ecclesial Movements and New Communities: The Response of the Holy Spirit to Today's Challenge of Evangelization*, Congregation for the Laity, 2006, 4.

> "The remarkable thing about gratitude is that it naturally and almost automatically grows and tends toward an ever-greater unselfishness. It begins rather egocentrically: I have received a gift that makes me happy. My gratitude is kindled by the fact that one of my needs has been satisfied, that one of my wishes has been fulfilled. But as soon as I begin to give thanks, my attention, which was at first fixed on myself, turns toward my benefactor. The emphasis, which before was on me, is transplanted little by little to another. I thank you because of what you have given me. I thank you because you are so good to me. I thank you because you are so good that it could occur to you to think of me. I thank you because you are so wonderful. I become more and more freed from myself and ever more fascinated by the love of the other. It begins with me and ends with you."[128]

An entire new school of psychology today has been founded on the power of gratitude. It is crazy how a little bit of gratitude can change our life and open us to self-gift. This idea of thanksgiving was not foreign to the early Christians and nor should it be to us: "As you therefore have received Christ Jesus the Lord, continue to live your life in him, rooted and built up in him and established in the faith, just as you were taught, abounding in thanksgiving" (Colossians 2:6-7). Be thankful!

Small Group Questions:
1. Why are we not more grateful with the many blessings in our life? Where does such blindness come from?

Going Deeper: Name some concrete ways to nurture a greater spirit of gratitude in your life.

---

[128] Stinnisen, *Holy Spirit, Fire of Divine Love*, 56.

NOTES

EPILOGUE

Regnum Christi and Integral Formation

It all sounds great on paper, right? Yet, reality can be a downer. Still, hope is possible! We need to hope again in love, in that genuine integrated love of the head and heart. It is the Gospel message that calls us to this love. The great English convert G. K. Chesterton once said, "It is not that the Gospel has been tried and found unwanted; no, it has been untried and found difficult." The message of the Gospel is challenging, but when embraced it releases our deepest human possibilities. Yet today, how many are ignorant of or dissuaded from this message, and hence make only a nominal effort to respond? Discouragement is the guillotine of heroic men and women. The proclamation of the Gospel to the world is exactly this: to believe there is a feast that corresponds to the deepest yearnings of our heart!

Optimism is at the heart of my spiritual family, Regnum Christi, an ecclesial movement in the Catholic Church.[129] Like many families today, we suffered a terrible humiliation within our own family, when we learned of our founder's duplicity. We can identify with the brokenness and the temptation to fall into discouragement. Such a crisis forces one to trust and to believe in hope again, to dream about the possibilities of a life redeemed and made new in Christ. He is mercy. He is goodness. His love *does* fill. Redemption in Christ is for real. Convinced of the power of Christ and his redemptive grace, St. John Paul II said, "that

---

[129] What are ecclesial movements? They are new spiritual families in the Catholic Church, true "laboratories of faith" that God has raised up for these times. They are authentic schools of Christian life, holiness, and mission. See Rylko, *Ecclesial Movements and New Communities*, footnote 118.

redemption is a truth, a reality, in the name of which man must feel himself called, and called with effectiveness."[130]

The philosophy of Regnum Christi makes integrated love a possible goal because it is rooted in the formation of the new man and new woman in Christ. We believe that God wants to touch and transform every corner of a person's soul and experience. Our mission is to try to provide experiences and quality resources to help make that happen. The integral formation that Regnum Christi proposes embraces all five of the components just outlined above: reflection, transforming grace, life-giving relationships, life-giving behavior, and gratitude. It fits them into four categories of integral formation: ***pray, learn, grow, and go!***[131] These are building blocks that shape an integrated human being—reason, will, emotions—the whole human person, so that he or she may flourish.

1. The "Pray" category reaches into our spiritual life and gives us tools to keep fresh our relationship with God.
2. The "Learn" category addresses the mind and heart, trying to help us expand and deepen our knowledge of God's plan for our own life, for the Church, and for the world.
3. The "Grow" category looks to help encourage the heart, inspiring us not only to pray and think about living life to the full, but to be intentional in growing in wisdom and virtue.
4. Finally, the "Go" category points to creative ideas, models, and opportunities for sharing the joy of our new discoveries.

---

130 St. John Paul II, *Theology of the Body*, 46, 4.
131 See www.RCspirituality.org for more information.

These four sectors help connect the head with the heart so we can love with that total self-gift—our life purpose!

When we anchor our life purpose in the commandment of love, "love one another as I have loved you" (John 15:12), it becomes a mission to bring meaning and purpose back to people who have lost hope. These four sectors embody what we in Regnum Christi call the integral formation of the human person. It is a calling to live a particular Christian lifestyle, awakening in the heart the desire to be witnesses of *another* way to live life. It is the way to happiness and fulfillment: the way of love. It is an urgent mission motivated by time and eternity, because "our mortality helps us realize that we have only a limited time in which to bring our lives to fulfillment" (*CCC* 1007). "Eternal life is not an unending succession of days on the calendar; it is a supreme moment of satisfaction. When totality embraces us, and we embrace it."[132] Christ is that totality and invites us to share him with the world!

---

132 Pope Benedict XVI, *Spe Salvi*, 12.

KEY TERMS AND DEFINITIONS[133]

Chastity: The right ordering of sexuality, body and spirit, which makes authentic self-giving love possible. This virtue is to be practiced by all Christians, whatever their state in life. For the unmarried, chastity entails abstinence from sex; for the married, chastity means that all sexual desires and behaviors are a sincere expression of the marriage covenant.

Communion of Persons: The kind of intimate union that can exist between persons only through a sincere and mutual gift of self.

Concupiscence: A disorder in our desires that inclines us toward sin. It is not a sin in itself.

Conscience: The practical judgment of our reason, judging a concrete action as either good or bad before, during, or after the action. It is the secret core of the human heart, the messenger of God, that bids the person, at the appropriate moment, to do good and to avoid evil.

Emotion: Psychic movements within the human person which produce motion and energy to help us in life.

Emotional Chastity: The habit that harmonizes the head and heart, and directs them towards the good of the other, in order to love authentically.

Eros: Romantic or sexual desire for a person of the opposite sex. It is part of the God-given interior force that attracts us to all that is good, true, and beautiful.

Free Will: Human beings' unique ability to make free choices. The faculty of our will is the motor that moves us down that pathway of choosing the good. In the end, *the good* is what we desire in all our willing.

Freedom for Excellence: The notion that our freedom is a gift, rooted in our natural inclination to know truth and choose it as

---

[133] A thank you to Bill Donaghy from the Theology of the Body Institute for his help with these terms and definitions.

a good for us. This concept of freedom best reflects our dignity and self-respect, without reducing it to blind impulse nor mere external pressure.

Freedom from Restriction: The common notion given to the word freedom, that anything that might inhibit our capacity to choose whatever we want is a negative. The mere arbitrary power *to choose* appears to be the *essence* of this freedom and it is centered wholly on the fact that one can choose "whatever I want, whether it is good or evil."

Goodwill-Love: According to St. John Paul II, human love matures to a third stage called goodwill-love. Love as goodwill seeks the good of the other and is free of self-interest. It is not a "I long for you as a good," but rather, "I long for *your* good."

Human Reason: The power of the mind to think, understand, and form judgments by a process of logic. Loosely speaking, human reason has two mental-power sources that feed it so that we can understand the world around us. First is discursive reason, which receives information so our mind can process, relate, analyze, and judge what it receives through the senses, and understand it. The second mental-power source is intuition. It is less active, more passive. Our intuitive mind perceives and receives its knowledge from sources such as nature, the arts, and faith, directly from God through the spirit independent of any active reasoning process.

Intentional Gratitude: When the habit of gratitude breaks us free from a me-centered mindset and leads us to an other-centered mindset.

Interior Freedom of the Gift: The ability to give oneself to another in sincere love and purity, through self-mastery made possible by Christ's redemption.

Language of the Body: The way a person "speaks" through the gestures and actions of the body, which tell either truth or lies. This communication is deeper than "body language" in the psychological sense.

Key Terms and Definitions

Life-Giving Behavior: The result of living your mission in life by loving well and putting your gifts at the service of your neighbor and the world.

Lust: Indulging of one's sexual desires while treating oneself or someone else as an object rather than as a person.

Moral Good/Evil: A person is moral when he or she exhibits goodness in his or her free actions. Moral good is that which fosters in the person *being* more, living more fully, and growing in one's possibilities. Moral evil is that which puts limits on human beings and contracts human life, extinguishing joy.

Narcissism: Excessive interest in or admiration of oneself.

Natural Law: The understanding of good and evil based on human reason that is inscribed in every human person.

Original Sin: The sin by which our first parents disobeyed God's commandment, choosing to follow their own will instead of God's will. All human beings inherit the resultant fallen state and loss of original holiness.

Person: A being with the capacity to know and to act freely, called to communion with other persons through a sincere gift of self. Each person is a unique and unrepeatable image of God.

Personalistic Norm: A concept that comes from the philosophy of St. John Paul II that begins with the all-important question "What is a person?" and the radical uniqueness of persons as distinct from every other kind of being. The personalistic norm states that a human being is the kind of good that is incompatible to being used; a person is that kind of good to which the only proper response is love.

Purity of Heart: The freedom to see the body in its true dignity as an expression of the inner person rather than as an object for the satisfaction of one's own desires. It is a virtue acquired by practicing temperance, but also a gift of the Holy Spirit.

Redemption: The action of saving or being saved from sin, error, or evil. The use of the word redemption in the New Testament Bible includes this same idea. Every person is weak and sinful and tends towards selfishness. Only through the price Jesus paid on the Cross is a sinful person redeemed from sin and death and restored to friendship with God.

Sacrament: A visible sign of an invisible reality. In the more specific sense, the seven sacraments are the signs instituted by Christ and administered by the Church, which signify and confer grace.

Secular: Denotes attitudes that are irreligious.

Self-Gift Love: Love that is a gift of *the whole* self, head and heart, making love fully human and bringing true fulfillment. It is through the gift of ourselves that we discover ourselves.

Self-Possession: The full mastery of our drives, passions, and motivations together with a conscious understanding of one's responsibility toward seeking the good of the other person.

Shame: There is good shame and bad shame. Bad shame is the distress and tension created by treating another person, or being treated, as a mere object for use rather than as a gift to be honored and loved. Good shame has the positive function of protecting the body from being so treated.

Spousal Meaning of the Body: The ability of the human body, in its masculinity or femininity, to express and realize our call to a communion of persons through self-giving love.

Theology of the Body: St. John Paul II's series of reflections on the meaning of the human person, love, sex, and marriage in light of the body. These talks were given in his general audiences between 1979 to 1984. These reflections, rooted in Scripture, recognize the fact that we do not just have bodies but are body-persons, whose inner life is expressed through the body.

Virtue: A habitual and firm disposition to do what is good, brought about either by repeated action or by a gift of grace.

ANSWERS TO SMALL GROUP QUESTIONS:

Chapter One: Two Words – Emotion and Chastity
1. Emotions are the psychic movements within the human person which produce motion and energy to help us in life. Chastity is the right ordering of sexuality, body and spirit, which makes authentic self-gift love possible. Emotional chastity is the habit that harmonizes the head and heart, and directs them towards the good of the other, in order to love authentically.
2. On the one hand, the culture affirms that we listen to our emotions and see them almost as intuitive powers, justifying doing away with caution and quickly leading us to think, say, or do what we feel. On the other hand, our culture can view emotions as a sign of weakness and immaturity. The word chastity comes with much misunderstanding today. Some have never heard of it; others mistakenly believe it is the repression of our desires or emotions to conform to outdated moral rules.

St. John Paul II and Emotional Chastity
1. St. John Paul II said that love is self-gift, that is, a *whole* person freely giving himself to another: body *and* soul.
2. St. John Paul II never used the exact term emotional chastity, in his writings. His efforts to explore a more complete definition of human love led some of his followers to coin the phrase emotional chastity.

Self-Possession
1. "You can't give what you don't got." Our happiness is bound up with our capacity to give ourselves to another, in other

words, to love. We grow in our self-knowledge the more we learn to serve the other.
2. Self-possession empowers us to take responsibility for our own actions and for the good of others. To love is truly a responsibility we inherit by simply being human. Our deepest human fulfillment depends on it.
3. False self-possession is based on strong pervasive materialistic influences. It treats the person and above all the human body like any other material object to be owned, controlled, or possessed. True self-possession sees the whole body-person reality as sacred, as a gift to be respected and esteemed.

The Feelings Revolution
1. The feelings revolution resulted in an extreme view that any repression of our emotions and feelings was detrimental to our emotional health. This brought forth an unfounded belief that any form of *self-restraint* was an invitation to neuroses or forms of phobia.
2. Feelings and emotions are very powerful when it comes to human love. It would not be surprising that the greatest negative effect of the feelings revolution was expressed in the area of human sexuality, where emotions tend to be most consequential.

Living Emotional Chastity
1. Emotional chastity is not just about good choices, but choices that deal with the nobility of the human person. Our greatest gift and mission in life is to love. The consistent good choice of gift of self in love to another brings ultimate happiness.
2. The current generation insightfully knows the difference between authenticity and duplicity. It has clearly identified a need to be accompanied in the journey of life by others

Chapter Two: Who Am I?

Human Dignity
1. The human person is a little world gathering all other worlds. Like animals, we feel pain and pleasure, and we have instincts. These are bodily, material characteristics. Like angels, but different, we know the truth and desire the good. These are our spiritual characteristics. Yet we are neither mere body nor just spirit. We are a unity of both. We are persons.
2. We have a higher purpose because we are made in the image of God. Our unique spiritual powers and our capacity for relationship image God. Our dignity flows from our ability to behave "in the image of God."

The Higher Purpose: Love
1. God is love and created us to love. Love is our special dignity and higher purpose. It is the fundamental and innate calling of every human being (*CCC* 1604).
2. Remembering that God is love, we realize that the strongest evidence that we are made in the image of the Trinity is that love alone makes us happy. Because we live in relationships, we live to love and to be loved. What God is, in himself, points to the inner calling of each of us as his creatures to be a gift to the other.

Human Reason
1. Human beings have the unique ability to reason. Animals do not. For example, human beings can reflect on their lives and relationships; they can compose music; they can choose

to love another person. Animals do not do any of these because they do not have the capacity for it.
2. Some basic universal truths common to all are: the respect for the value of life, the begetting and raising of children, intellectual knowledge, and play or recreation.
3. One could say that our mind functions in two ways. First, from the external material world, our mind processes, relates, analyzes, and judges what it receives through the senses to understand it. We can call this the discursive mind. Second, from the internal world, our intuitive world processes experience without any effort from our active discursive reason. We call this intuition. The intuitive mind *perceives and receives* the power of human experience, independent of any active reasoning process.

The Will
1. *The good* is what we desire in all our willing or choosing. The good that the will chooses is what is loveable or desirable. It is that which engages and attracts our entire person.
2. "Ought" points to full, fuller, and fullest being, that is, the deep-down desire *to be* the finest possible human being. We value this *particular good* as helping us be *more* or *better* persons.
3. The human will should not be seen as the absolute "decider." The will is meant to be trained to see, with the help of reason, the good of our emotions, and to help rule over them democratically.

How Reason and Will Work Together
1. The will is like a motor with no light, and reason is like a light with no motor. Within each person, reason and will need each other so as to work together to "see" (reason) and to "move" (will) toward the right and true end.

2. When these three dimensions (reason, will, emotions) are integrated and are active and cooperating, the human person is truly free and flourishes. When they are not working together the person can be enslaved.

Freedom
1. Freedom is a gift from God, but it is not an absolute gift. *Freedom from restriction* is a common view of freedom today that sees as negative anything that might inhibit our capacity to choose whatever we want. The mere arbitrary power to choose appears to be the essence of this freedom, even choosing something evil. However, this apparent unconstrained freedom is impossible: human freedom will always have boundaries because we are finite, limited creatures.
2. *Freedom for excellence* is rooted in the light of our reason that allows to see the good of our emotions and helps us to "feel" fully before choosing a course of action. Reason acknowledges our feelings and brings us to that good which will help us most flourish. *Freedom for excellence* best reflects our dignity and self-respect without reducing it to blind impulse nor mere external pressure. It is about knowing and choosing a greater good in the power of our emotional state. Love by its nature must be free. If our love is somehow inhibited or even enslaved by something, then it is not true love—whether we are aware of this or not.

Conscience
1. Conscience is that secret core of the human heart, the messenger of God, that bids the person, at the appropriate moment, to do good and to avoid evil. I am free to act or not on the voice of conscience. Yet we are responsible for educating our conscience: seeking to know and do the right thing, what is just and good.

2. Family or community life is that system of forces that reinforces the person we are becoming. When the right standards are affirmed in our family consistently over time, they also form the right behaviors. The healthy and consistent giving and receiving of love in family and friendship is the critical training ground for healthy mature human flourishing.
3. We form our conscience when we commit ourselves to listening to quality and healthy sources of truth, goodness, and beauty, for example, building friendships with people who love us and challenge us to be the best we can. However, we can deform our conscience by exposing ourselves to the values of a culture that go contrary to human flourishing: the superficial empty values of a passing age transmitted through the media, politics, fashion, entertainment, and financial concerns.

Moral Beings
1. To be human is to be a moral being. It is to have inborn standards of conscience that guide our thinking and acting towards what is good and right over what is wrong. When we say a person is moral, it means that he or she exhibits goodness in free actions.
2. Choosing the moral good *expands* your life and your heart, bringing joy, peace, and fulfillment. Choosing moral evil, rather, *contracts* your life, making the heart heavy, extinguishing the joy.
3. The concept of the *perfectibility* of the person is based in the fact that we perfect ourselves by our good choices. This is not some sort of self-creation or the inventing of what is important and not important to us. Love as self-gift is *the one choice* that perfects us the most.

Human Sexuality
1. Our human sexuality is more than just physical acts. It communicates a great mystery. The *invisible* mystery of God's interpersonal love has become *visible* in the physical human world for us to see, concretely through the human body.
2. Our male to female body-person design expresses *being a gift* to the other, particularly in the marital act. God so designed our bodies that this physical act of human love speaks of a total self-giving. And this act reflects who *he* is the source and essence of self-gift love. St. John Paul II calls this the spousal language of the body.
3. Today most people wrongly reduce the word *sex* or *sexual* to mean only one thing: *genital behavior*. Human sexuality is ultimately the power of sharing oneself. It is *human*, and not identical to the animalistic drive found in subhuman species. We humans can share our very selves with another. Only humans can be sexual in this manner.

Chapter Three: Our Emotional World

The Place of Emotions in the Human Person
1. Our emotions are like motors because they cause us to move. They are a response to whatever information our senses provide concerning the goodness, lack of goodness, usefulness, or harmfulness that things have for us. Our emotions are part of our human existence whereby man senses the good and perceives evil.
2. To authentically love with our whole selves requires the healthy contribution of our emotions! To love merely from our intelligence (the head), and not include our emotions, can be hazardous, even dangerous. It will translate into a human love that is incomplete.

Emotions: What Do I Do with Them?

1. Our emotions can cause us all sorts of problems when we think they "own us." They do not. Negative emotions often translate into "I am not a good person." The integration of our emotional world begins by understanding that our understanding that they are part of who we are. But they do not control us. *They are not us.* We need to avoid labeling ourselves in unhealthy ways because of struggles with negative emotions.
2. Among the repercussions of suppressing emotion, we have the self-medicating habit of displacing emotion through pleasure-seeking. We evade negative emotions by seeking gratification to numb how we feel. Suppressing emotion also tends to shut down *all feelings* —the negative and the positive. The "stuffing" of our emotional world takes up a lot of energy. This constant management of our emotions keeps us from being able to freely say yes to so many other amazing opportunities that life offers.
3. Since our emotions can react in milliseconds, it is very important to be able to give space to your thoughts to catch up. True mindfulness is all about this pausing, processing, and reflecting before acting to avoid blind impulse or unrefined emotion. Developing the habitual application to this mindful process allows one to respond rather than simply react.

The Case of Anger

1. All anger is not negative. Anger can be the emotion that fuels one to overcome great obstacles like fighting injustice and evil. Justified anger set in the right course by both reason (head) and love (heart) can be a catalyst for inspiring service to others. Despite anger's emotional intensity, we still have freedom of choice. We have the capacity to use that energy in a positive, rather than a negative, way.

2. It is never good to suppress your emotions. We need to allow ourselves to *feel the feeling*, not repress it or pretend that it is not there. Recognize and be aware of the emotion. Do not repress it. Nonetheless, beware of what you *do* with it because this choice could be hurting you, others, and God.
3. The intensity of anger can blind us to what is right and good in a given moment. Having the presence of mind to wait and allow the light of reason to shed clarity on the situation helps lead our stronger emotions to their best and most fruitful end.

The Uniqueness of Shame
1. Good shame is that normal emotion that gives us permission to be human by making us aware of our limits and maintaining our human boundaries. Bad shame is the inability to let go of guilt of the past, forgive oneself, and live in the present.
2. The creation story in the book of Genesis narrates Adam's "fall from innocence" and the reveals the nature of sexual shame. The words "I was afraid, because I was naked" (Genesis 3:10) reveal a break in the original spiritual and physical unity of man. The original harmony inside man and with those around him is disturbed due to sin. Something within the body is now at war with the spirit. The unity of the person is threatened.
3. Shameful feelings are like the light on the car's dashboard blinking when something is not quite right with the car. Sexual shame is that blinking light in us, part of the wiring of the human person, that beckons the question, "Are we hurting ourselves and others?"

Emotions and the Heart
1. The heart is the interior "headquarters" of the person, "the dwelling place where we live." The heart is the culmination of our very being–spiritual, emotional, physical–the fullness

of how we were created in God's image and likeness. Emotions, on the other hand, are inherently bodily and are accompanied by bodily processes.
2. Pausing when our hearts are agitated is a wise practice. One of the key principles for making good choices is *never act* when you find yourself in a moment of interior desolation or angst. It is precisely this thoughtful pausing before the movements of the heart that refines our thinking and brings a sense of balance to our lives.

Heart-Intuition
1. The heart speaks to what is important to us. According to St. John Paul II, the heart-intuition is like an echo in each of us of the original beginning, when man and woman were first created for total love. The head and the heart were in perfect unison; a true knowing of the goodness of the other and a pure desire to honor it.
2. Sin has almost silenced the echo, but it did not completely silence it. We have become estranged from God and are at odds to that interior calling to be true to love as a total self-gift.
3. When we experience genuine love in and around us, we begin to hear again the faint echo of the original calling within us. In other words, only if we see it, feel it, and practically touch it, does it stir in us that slumbering heart-intuition of a renewed belief that such love *does* exists. When relationships are centered on authentic love as self-gift, they build us up, affirms us, and inspires us to want the same for our own lives.

Love Doesn't Always "Feel" Good
1. Suffering and love must go together. When we say "yes" to love, we also say "yes" to being open to the other and to the possibility of being hurt by the other. It is a letting go of myself and its selfish ways for the other, allowing myself to be pruned, even wounded. Christ shows us the way.

He opens himself to love through his Passion and Cross to show that we can also reach the Resurrection (peace, love, and divine beatitude).
2. The martyrs follow Christ and show us how to embrace the pedagogy of love. They have found the truth about life and love in the encounter with Christ, and nothing and no one could ever change this. Their attitude teaches us that in all love, human or Divine, there is nothing lost through sacrifice.
3. We all understand the importance of going to the gym and getting regular exercise. It helps the body to be more productive. In a similar way, daily sacrifice helps us be better lovers and better human beings. When we are courageous enough to embrace the sacrifices that come our way, then such love is roused and expands to stretch itself in new ways for others, bringing great fruitfulness.

Chapter Four: Progression of Love
1. Like anything in the natural world there are laws of maturity and growth. Love is no different. As one learns to practice an ever-maturing love that demands "all of me" in favor of what is more naturally appealing, the steps of growth are marked by imperfection and failure. Any good habit takes time and a lot of effort.
2. Emotional chastity nurtures a healthy maturing of love centered on the dignity of the other person. It is a channeling of our positive dispositions, the moderation of our selfish tendencies, and the steady improving of our personal efforts to express unselfish love in thought, word, and deed.

First Stage: Love as Attraction
1. The "raw material" of attraction-love is the initial good that attracts us to something good about this other someone. This particular good of the other is based in the sensual

values of the person, for example, a nice smile, a good sense of humor, and beautiful eyes.
2. Attraction does not equal love. We are free to act or not act on that attraction. Attraction-love may draw us to something particularly characteristic of the other, but that quality that we are attracted to is attached to *a person*, and the whole of this person deserves to be respected. Authentic love involves the whole person and not just the parts that I like.
3. Our emotions do not possess an intellectual *power*; that is, they are not concerned about knowing the whole truth of the other person. They "see" only partially. Our emotions can falsify attraction, perceiving a value that might not even be present. Obviously, this can be very dangerous for new love. Reason helps enlighten us to the fact that emotion is *not* a measurement of love, but rather it is a mature responsible response towards the other.

Second Stage: Love as Desire
1. Desire-love communicates, "I want you because you are a good for me." This person fulfills a need that I have. Since love as desire implies the filling of the other's needs, completing what is incomplete, great care needs to be given not to make this desire-love a reason to "use" the other for selfish personal ends.
2. As human beings, we have a unique gift to be able to consciously reflect before we react. There is freedom to choose at this stage of love, and therefore we are free to respond or not respond to such intense emotions.
3. Emotional chastity allows the natural course of emotional connection to take place, but monitors that connection with the precision of reason, moving from the tendency to focus on a specific quality to focus on the value of the whole person. This is not the repression of desires.

Third Stage: Love as Goodwill
1. Goodwill-love is free of self-interest. It is "I long for *your* good." There is no personal consideration or ulterior motives.
2. Goodwill-love can be present when a couple decides to cohabitate. However, cohabitation, being a commitment to non-commitment, very often can begin to or quickly slide into a relationship of convenience and self-interest. This does not reflect the bilateral nature of goodwill-love. Reciprocity must be present for goodwill-love to come to maturity.

Fourth Stage: Love as Unconditional
1. Unconditional love perfects the persons who experience it, and brings the subject and object of that love the greatest fulfillment. It is truly the unification of persons—going from "I" to "we "and the surrendering of one's "I." It is the sharing of one's own person with another. None of the other stages of human love can take a human being on his quest for the good of the other as does love as self-gift.
2. When a couple has a shared orientation towards a common ideal of marriage, they begin their life together with a total YES to this ideal. Putting off living together before marriage is already a shared sacrifice that both make, a shared act of love of waiting for something so good, until God and the community blesses it. This dynamic of generous and sacrificial self-gift is the best preparation for marriage in order to build your relationship on rock.
3. Contraception and cohabitation are built on distrust. Both the marital act of total self-gift and the public declaration of vows in marriage express this total trust. "I hold nothing back and give myself totally to you—body and soul. "I vow to you before God and my dearest family and friends to love you in good times or bad, sickness or health...." This is a different mindset from the couple who contracepts or

cohabitates and finds themselves often in fear, calculation, and distrust of one another and of God.

Chapter Five: What Love Is NOT

1. *Innate* means simply that to love is natural to us. It is the proper behavior of human beings. We are wired for it.
2. Human beings live in relationship because God is first a relationship. God is a family, Divine love from which flows the Trinity, a family of persons (Father, Son, and Holy Spirit).
3. God has placed in the human heart a hunger for perfect love. However, nothing human, nothing from this world, can fill it. Knowing this human dilemma, God became man to answer this desire of love in our hearts. Jesus Christ, true God and true man, is the perfect lover who fills our hunger. "I have come to bring you life and life to the full" (John 10:10).

Chapter Six: What Inhibits Living Emotional Chastity?

Human Frailty

1. We know that we are not perfect and make mistakes. Our love can have selfish motives.
2. Sin is the possibility of rebellion, of refusal, of rejection of God. Perhaps rejection of the concept of sin today is just one more manifestation of the human tendency to disobey and rebel against any authority.

Dehumanizing Secular Culture

The Materializing of Love

1. Secular culture is irreligious. It is a culture imploding on itself because the sense of God and the dignity of his creation, particularly the human person, is of no importance.

2. The "materializing of love" is a description of the secular "disposable" culture and its influence on human love. Such materialistic influences are so strong that even human beings fall into the material categories of use and discard, with a total disregard for their dignity.

The Cycle of Using
1. The "cycle of using" is a strong tendency in relationships to seek a certain emotional experience; once it is reached and loses its luster, the cycle starts again. The cycle looks different in men and women. Though for one it may be more physical and the other more emotional, both are seeking some form of gratification at the expense of the other.
2. Lust has different disordered expressions in men and women. Generally, for men it is externalized: the gawking at a woman's body, the vulgar verbalization of the same, and the acting out of what is seen in movies or pornography. For a woman, on the other hand, it is internal: thoughts, imagination, and the illusion of love.

The Lie of Absolute Freedom
1. The false notion of freedom today sees itself as something almost absolute: Any guidelines that obstruct our freedom to choose are negative. True freedom knows that with every choice one sacrifices something.
2. There are probably many reasons why people are reluctant about long-term commitments. One might be the tendency today to get caught up in "the fear of missing out." Long-term relationships demand investment and sacrifice, but if we have little positive experience of this in our lives, fear might paralyze us from taking the step with confidence.
3. Some examples to discuss are, for example, "I like the freedom to work from home, but I don't like the deadlines that are put on me." "I like the freedom to travel, but not

necessarily the responsibility that comes with paying the bills." "I like the freedom to be able to have sex with my significant other, but not the serious responsibility that comes with having a child."

The Reality of Evil
1. Evil is the wicked forces in the world that are against the good of the human person and ultimately God the Creator.
2. What God has created is essentially good. Evil is the active force that works contrary to God and perverts that good he created. For example, it is good and natural for men and women to be attracted to one another. Lust is the twisting of that good into something that is perverted and unhealthy, allowing us to hurt one another.

Chapter Seven: Redemption
1. The word "redemption" also means to *restore*. Christ's redemption restores the original unity to man and to woman that was lost by sin. This restoration allows our human family and our relationships with one another to be seen as a gift rather than as a threat.
2. Christian baptism calls us to imitate Christ. Christ discipled his first apostles. He accompanied them on their gradual conversion as they conformed their lives to his life. To be discipled and to disciple others is central to our calling to follow Christ.

Baptism and the Power of Redeeming Grace
1. The three new powers we receive at baptism are faith, hope, and love. The power of our intellect is given the gift of faith to know truth in a new way, and the power of our will is given the gift of hope and love to love in a new way.
2. The new powers of faith, hope, and love *reorder* and *reintegrate* the human person. Redeeming grace brings "light"

to our reason, "strength" to our will, and "order" to our emotions. All of me has been redeemed! This process of reordering happens according to Christ's dominion in your life. The more his authority grows in breadth and extension into every corner of your life, the quicker the transformation happens.

Chapter Eight: Living Emotional Chastity: The Law of Gradualness

1. The law of gradualness with regard to forming habits simply means that habits take time to form. Habits progress through stages marked by imperfection and human weakness. Good habits, like the virtue of chastity, grow over time. They require repetition. We *gradually* form the good habit of being chaste in our thoughts, words, and deeds.
2. Some typical pitfalls are falling into pornography, allowing ourselves to choose inappropriate films or music that will affect us, or giving up on prayer and our dependence on God when things get tough.

Personal Reflection

1. The words of Socrates are an invitation to us to grow in our self-awareness. To know yourself is to know your weaknesses. Living emotional chastity is an invitation into this journey of self-knowledge.

Sacramental Life

1. The sacraments are outward signs of inward grace. Christ instituted the sacraments, to reach our very humanity–reason, will, emotions–through what most speaks to us. These signs are visible and intelligible to our senses and communicate grace to us. God is not distant but right there with us in our human experience.

2. The Holy Eucharist and Reconciliation are not just *curative* medicine to help heal the soul from sin, but also *preventative* medicine. They help us build resistance to sin like vitamins build up resistance to disease. When living a sacramental life is consistent, so is our love. The strength of a more loving spirit is given by God's medicinal grace through the sacraments.
3. A regular commitment to prayer and the sacramental life will begin to heal us of our pride, our vanity, and our laziness. Grace will illuminate the inner voice of conscience to our weaknesses and will show us the areas in our life where love needs perfecting. If we persevere in this commitment, we become different people, true followers of Christ.

Life-Giving Relationships
1. Life-giving relationships are those relationships with people who inspire us, encourage us, and challenge us to be better. The example of these types of people helps us assimilate the right way to treat others. In other words, we learn the art of self-gift love. Life-giving relationships are examples for us of how authentic love should look. If we are treated a certain way that is truly loving, then most likely we will try to imitate this way with others.
2. To be a good friend to another is to seek the best for the other. Important characteristics of a true friend are honesty, transparency, and holding the other to the right standards. Trust and discretion are critical in friendship, particularly for more intimate and personal issues.

Life-Giving Behavior
1. Life-giving behavior means loving your neighbors by serving them. When we seek to serve others, it communicates to them that they are important and appreciated.

2. Serving the other means your attention is not on your needs, but on someone else's. The experience of serving others has the power not just to affirm those whom you serve, but contains within it the power of "self-affirmation" as well.

The Power of Intentional Gratitude
1. The general lack of gratitude in all of us shows our tendency to be self-serving. It is no doubt another ugly consequence of our fallen human nature. Love and gratitude are similar in that both are crucial to our happiness, and yet we are not very good at either. They are habits that need nurturing.

APPENDICES

APPENDIX I: HELPFUL TIPS FOR SILENCE

Silence *intentionally embraced* equals solitude. Then again, solitude is not sitting there in the dark somewhere in your house waiting for something to happen. Rather it is a door to listening to the echo of your heart connect with the echo of *the Other*—with or without words. It brings sense to us because it brings us into a relationship with a personal God, who speaks to us in the echo of our longings for him. A change in our very thinking happens:

Here are some ways to find more mindfulness in your life by finding more silence:

- Set personal boundaries on your use of social media and pick moments during the week/month where you "phone/media fast." Pair up with someone so you can be accountable to one another on this commitment.
- Consider getting an app that helps set boundaries on the use of IT in your life. The principle is that freedom from the internet is so rare and exotic and practically impossible that it is becoming a commodity. We have to buy peace.
- Write in a journal. In addition to allowing you to express yourself, this can help you become more self-aware and hold yourself accountable. Recognize your urges to break the silence. This may help you learn a lot about yourself.
- Buy an alarm clock and wake up to it rather than your phone, thus giving your first thoughts to something else rather than your phone.
- Drive with no music in the car for all or at least part of the time.

- Put paper on your desk and write "be quiet" or "silence is golden" or other words that can remind you to cultivate silence.
- Don't speak so that you learn to listen. You may notice that you often say what's on your mind before listening to what others have to say. Try to stay silent for an entire day, to get better at listening before you speak.
- Commit to going for a walk (with no headphones!) in your community, at your local park, or further from home for a longer trek during the weekend.
- Schedule an annual spiritual retreat (the more silence the better!) and allow for some much-needed digital detoxing.
- Plan a vacation that exposes yourself (and family) to more silence and solitude: Go to the mountains or someplace more remote.

APPENDIX II: THOUGHT MANAGEMENT

Today's mantra of taking *responsibility for your mental health* is not too far off the mark. Here are some practical suggestions on doing just that in your daily life:

- Junk-proof your mind. Avoid reading or exposing your mind to anything that is mental junk food: trashy gossip magazines, provocative websites, news sites, and blogs.
- Be discerning in your choice of music. Music has a particular power over the human heart and can lead the emotions in all sorts of directions—not always healthy directions.
- Foster thinking that is positive and hope-filled. This is not a disposition most of us naturally possess. It is a *decision*. Regular prayerful reflection helps this.
- For those who experience a vibrant emotional world, recognize that this is a gift, not a curse. Acknowledge the negative emotions that consume your thinking. Limit the sharing of your emotions with just anyone—exercise self-control! Share your emotions only with trusted friends.
- Cultivate a spirit of forgiveness: Let go of the hurts that you may experience. Give people the benefit of the doubt. Peace comes only when there is forgiveness.
- Affirm God's goodness and blessings—including the crosses we face! Gratitude calms.

Made in the USA
Monee, IL
24 September 2020